FATHERS RAISING DAUGHTERS

FATHERS RAISING DAUGHTERS

THE FATHER'S GUIDE TO THE FEMALE MIND-FIELD

NIGEL LATTA

 HarperCollins*Publishers*

National Library of New Zealand Cataloguing-in-Publication Data

Latta, Nigel, 1967-
Fathers raising daughters : the father's guide to the
female mind-field / Nigel Latta.
Includes bibliographical references.
ISBN 978-1-86950-787-9
1. Fathers and daughters. 2. Girls—Psychology. I. Title.
306.8742—dc 22

First published 2010
HarperCollins*Publishers* (New Zealand) Limited
P.O. Box 1, Auckland 1140

ISBN: 978 1 86950 787 9

Cover design by Natalie Winter
Cover image by Marc Debnam/Getty Images
Internal text typesetting by Island Bridge

Printed by Griffin Press, Australia

70gsm Classic used by HarperCollinsPublishers is a natural,
recyclable product made from wood grown in sustainable forests. The
manufacturing processes conform to the environmental regulations
in the country of origin, Finland.

Contents

Preface

Sugar and spice . . . and a little napalm

She looked as sweet as fake maple syrup, sitting there in her designer jeans and a pink top which showed far too much skin for a 13-year-old, but I'd been doing this long enough to know that books and covers have only a very loose association.

In the same way that it's true that if you're lost in the wilderness it's good to avoid the red berries because they're the ones most likely to be poisonous, beware the girly girls — they're the ones most likely to bite.

Her dad and mum had brought her in; although it would probably be more accurate to say that they'd dragged and cajoled her in with a mixture of threats, bribes, and begging. Mum was stuck in traffic, so at the moment it was just the three of us.

Kara, bless her, had recently discovered that she could get her way whenever she wanted simply through the infliction of grinding terror on her parents. She just wasn't old enough to appreciate that there might actually be a good reason why they got so terrified when she threatened to run away every time they tried to stand up to her incessant demands.

'So, Peter, I'm thinking that Amanda's going to be a while, so why don't we kick things off?' I said to her dad. 'What's brought you along today?'

Dad looked briefly at Kara, who duly rolled her eyes and slumped in her seat, looking as if she was both utterly disinterested and loving every moment of the drama: 'We've been having a few problems at home.'

Kara looked at him and affected a sustained, scornful, and well-practised sneer.

'How so?' I asked.

'We don't seem to be able to see eye-to-eye on anything.'

'*No*,' Kara cut in, and the venom in her voice would have made a death adder flinch. 'That's not true, Dad.'

'Well, we do seem to be arguing a lot these days.'

'So?'

'So it isn't very nice for me or your mum, and I'm sure it isn't very nice for—'

'Well if Mum wasn't such a *bitch* it wouldn't end up in an argument all the time.'

I could see that Kara was beginning to wind up. In my experience, 13-year-old girls are a little like dynamite that's been left lying around in the sun for too long: they start to leak gelignite after a while, and all it takes is a little bump and the whole lot goes up.

'Please don't talk about your mother like that,' Peter said.

For most of us, this would not constitute a bump. Peter said it firmly, but reasonably. He didn't swear at her, or threaten her, or even raise his voice. He even said 'please'. None of that mattered, though, because Kara was looking for any old reason, and that would do as well as anything else.

'*Fuck you!*' she said, leaping to her feet, bursting into tears, and affecting a martyr's stance all in one fell swoop. '*You're just the same as her. You always take her side and you never listen to me. Fuck you, then — I don't have to stay and listen to this.*'

Before Peter could say another word, she stormed out of the room, slamming the door hard enough to make the wall behind me shudder.

We both sat there for a moment as the dust, both literal and figurative, settled around us. Peter had a look on his face that I've seen many times over the years: a curious blend of bone-jarring confusion and complete dismay.

'Do you know where napalm gets its name?' I asked him. (One of the nice things about working with guys is you can assume that they know what napalm is.)

'Pardon?'

'Napalm. Do you know where it gets its name?'

He shook his head. 'No.'

'It actually comes from two of the ingredients they use to make the gasoline into a gel: naphthenic and palmitic salts. Na-palm.'

'Really?'

'Yeah. In fact, the naphthenic part comes from crude oil, and the palmitic bit is from plants, palm oil. They first used the stuff in the Second World War, on 17 July 1944 actually, when they dropped it on a fuel dump in France. And you know what the secret of good napalm is?'

'It has to be sticky,' replied Peter.

'Exactly,' I said, once again thinking how marvellous it was to work with men who knew about things like what makes napalm so special. 'Up until then, the problem had been that if they dropped incendiary bombs the stuff splashed all over the place and drained away too quickly. They needed something that would stick and burn.'

'I know how that feels,' he said. 'She napalms us all the time.'

'Raising a daughter can be a confusing thing,' I said as he slowly nodded in agreement. 'They tell you about all the sugar and spice, but no one tells you about the napalm.'

'Half the time I have no idea what's going on with her,' he said. 'It wasn't so bad when she was little, but now . . . good God. Why doesn't someone write a book that tells us poor confused dads what's going on inside a girl's head?'

'Well, actually,' I said, 'I'm doing that at the moment, and I'm thinking that you guys might be just the preface I was looking for.'

He laughed. 'So what's the book about?'

'It's like a dad's guide to raising girls. I explain why girls feel so different when actually they're not really, and some of the big do's and don'ts I've learned from all the dads and daughters I've seen over the years.'

'Such as?'

'Well, stuff like don't be a big girl, for one.'

Peter laughed again. 'What does that mean?'

'It means just because you have a girl it doesn't mean you need to be one to raise her.'

'Thank God,' he said. 'If I was more like her then our house would be little more than smoking ruins after a day or so.'

At that moment Amanda, who had resolved her traffic issues, walked into my office. 'Where's Kara?' she asked.

'Did you know that napalm is made from palm oil?' Peter asked her.

'Nay-what?' she said, looking puzzled.

Peter and I looked at each, smiling and enjoying the fraternity that only the manly sharing of technical information about incendiary bombs can produce.

It's a guy thing.

Interestingly, so is this book.

1

Zombies and high heels

Let's face it, for most of us the women in our lives are a total bloody mystery. We pretend that we understand them — because if we don't then it usually leads to trouble — but really they're pretty confusing. Why, for instance, do they delight in telling us over and over about all the many complex tasks they are able to undertake as part of their every day, things like getting the kids up, dressed, fed, homework done, hair and teeth brushed, bags packed, dropped at school, buying groceries whilst sticking to a budget, clothes washed and mended and replaced, doctors appointments, safe collection of children from school and subsequent dropping off at the correct after-school activities, more homework, evening meals prepared and dispensed, teeth brushed, stories read, children safely tucked into bed, various administrative tasks performed, and on top of all of this they tell us they can remember birthdays, favourite colours, teachers' names, friends' names, allergies, hairstyles, time of the next high tide and cycle of the moon, and all on top of working either part- or full-time . . . yet put them in front of a car with a flat tyre and they are struck dumb. If it's flat, then many women dial the Automobile Association, or their guy, or both.

Seriously, if they can multitask so well and do all that stuff, how come they have so much trouble with car tyres? It's not hard, is it? I mean, it's not rewiring the Space Shuttle or removing a tumour from someone's brain. It's as simple as jack the car up, undo lug-nuts, take bad tyre off, put good tyre on, tighten lug-nuts, let down jack.

Job done.

Just yesterday I received an amusing email to this very effect, suggesting a new series of *Survivor* where dads get left on an island with three kids and have to try to do all the things that mums do every day. It was circulating amongst my wife's friends, and they were having a jolly good :-) and even the odd ROFL about how clever mums are and how completely hopeless dads are. Now, to be fair, it was a funny email, and I did LOL myself at one point, but it constantly amazes me how much the fairer sex think they're the wiser sex by default.

A wise person does not wear high heels.

High heels are, without doubt, ridiculous pieces of footwear. You can barely walk in high heels, let alone run. I look at high heels and I always think how crazy it would be to wear something that not only makes your feet hurt, but also makes it virtually impossible to run away from zombies. I'm a guy, so I think about stuff like escaping from zombies. Women don't seem to think all that much about zombies which, I'm sure you'll agree, is a little short-sighted.

And I love it when women say that the reason they do that high heels, make-up and la-de-dah gig is all for us, for men. Apparently they wouldn't do it if we didn't expect them to.

Really?

You see, if women collectively issued a statement saying that they expected me to wear high heels, or a chicken suit, or even a fake plastic moustache, I'd just say no.

'We'd like you to wear silly shoes that hurt your feet,' they'd ask.

'No,' I'd say.

'Why not?' they'd ask.

'Zombies.'

'What?'

'Zombies. I'm not wearing those, because I can't run in them, which would be OK if the zombies are the slow, ambling British type, but if they turn out to be the really fast, really scary American type then I'd be lunch if I tried running in those things.'

They wouldn't understand.

Zombies and high heels: two things that just don't go together.

Men and women are quite different, right? Well, kind of, but we'll get to that in a little while. On the surface, though, it certainly seems there are a lot of things which back up the idea that we live on different planets.

Shopping is one. Most women love to shop. They don't even have to buy something. They just like looking. I hate looking. Most guys do. The only shops that are fun just to look in are bookstores and electronics stores. Everything else is a little sucky.

Another difference is the million variations on this conversation that take place in cafés, living rooms, bedrooms, and cars every single day when you ask that question we all end up asking:

'Are you angry with me?'

'No.'

'Are you sure, because you seem angry?'

'Well, I'm not.'

'Was it that thing I said about collecting the mail?'

'No.'

'Was it that I didn't put the dishes in the dishwasher this morning?'

'Nope.'

'Was it what I said on the phone to your dad this morning?'

'No, it wasn't that. Why would it be that? There was nothing wrong with what you said to him.'

Oh shit, you think. *It* was *what I said to her dad*. 'What? What did I say?'

'Nothing.'

'No, it's something. I know "nothing" and it isn't this. This is something.'

She shrugs.

Oh shit. 'I was perfectly polite on the phone. I didn't say anything in any shape or form that was in any way rude.'

'That's right,' she says, with that particular inflection in her tone that implies the kind of genial goodwill a boot has towards an ant. 'You didn't say *anything* wrong at all.'

Here's where you do that quick analysis, trying to work out what could possibly have occurred in what you had thought was a perfectly normal conversation that could have resulted in this clear and present danger.

And that's when you remember that you were watching something on the telly when your father-in-law called, and so you handed over the phone fairly quickly.

Finally, the penny drops.

'Is it because you think I was short with him on the phone?'

Nothing, just the stony silence which is how wives tell husbands, without the use of a single word, that finally we've figured it out.

Now all this is fine and well, because we love the women in our lives despite the fact they are often hard to fathom, and we accept the passing moments of leaden confusion as simply the cost of spending your life with someone else who isn't a guy. There's also the fact that in a relationship it's one-on-one, and so the odds at least seem to be fair.

But what about when you have a daughter? What then? For most dads in this situation, the thought which usually follows the knowledge that you're going to have a girl is the disturbing realization that now you will be outnumbered. You will now be a minority in your own life.

Forever.

Bugger.

Perhaps not surprisingly, there have been numerous studies that have shown that — at a general level — men prefer to have sons and women prefer to have daughters. Much of the theorizing around why this is revolves around ideas of each sex feeling more comfortable with their own kind. My theory is that it really isn't about any of that. I think it's all about the numbers. I think it's all about votes.

And why are votes important? Because when you're standing in the video store and the decision comes down to watching *Fluffy Barbie Fairy Lovey Dovey Pony Party Movie 2* or *Pirates of the Caribbean*, then votes count. It all comes down to a show of hands at that point, and if you're the minority then it's going to be some soppy movie about magic ponies and fairies and bloody Barbie.

If you're outnumbered in your house, then you simply have to accept the fact that you are going to have to suffer watching a lot of really dumb movies. Unfortunately there's nothing I can do about that. I could give you some sappy line about how, if you just give it a chance and approach the shared movie night with an open heart and a curious mind, you'll learn more about the world of girls, and it will be a moment to treasure.

It won't.

It'll just be an evening spent watching a really dumb movie.

So you're pretty much on your own with that particular aspect of raising girls. Everything else, though, we can do something about.

This book is not going to be a long book, so I'm not going to go on about things unnecessarily. The reason that I'm going to make this book short and (relatively speaking) to the point, is that this is a book for blokes, and we generally don't like a lot of flowery fluffing about. I don't; in fact, it irritates the shit out of me when people fluff about.

Get to the point dammit, is what I'm usually muttering inside my head.

If you're a dad raising a girl all by yourself, then this book is going to be particularly helpful for you. Parenting any kind of kid by yourself is hard work, but it's particularly difficult if you're raising a child who's on the other team. We all probably have a rough idea what boys are thinking and how they operate — but girls? Who can know what's going on inside a girl's head?

Luckily there are, at least in my humble opinion, a few basic principles you can follow to help you navigate your way through some of the more confusing-looking girl-stuff, and some helpful approaches to dig yourself out of a hole if you've already strayed off the course a little.

And the other part of all this is how do you manage the whole puberty thing if you're a guy raising girls? Well, relax (as much as you can about that one), because I'm going to go over all that in detail — probably in far more detail then you actually want to know, but it has to be done. You are going to need to know about 'woman stuff', and not just in theory, but the messier, unpleasant parts of it as well. If you're the one giving the 'birds and bees' talk, and more specifically the nitty-gritty of that 'time of the month' stuff, you're going to need to know how to do all that.

The other thing I'm going to do here is help you out if you're a dad reading this book under duress. I've been in the parenting-book racket long enough to know that the vast majority of the people who read parenting books are mums. Clearly there will be single dads who got here all by themselves, but there will also be a contingent of dads reading this book who didn't jump in voluntarily but were pushed. Usually what happens is that mum buys the book, reads it herself, and then reads aloud long sections to dad. If those bits are funny enough, and useful enough, dad will then have a read of the book himself. It isn't because we don't care, or we're not interested in our kids, I think it's just that dads have a different approach to raising kids. We tend to think that it can't be all that hard, and there isn't too much that can go wrong. Generally, that's pretty much true. Most of us get through, some with more scars than others, but we all tend to make it out the other side.

Having said all of that, it might well be that you've had this book plonked in front of you with the fairly obvious expectation that you'll read it. If that's the case, then I've made a special effort to make it really easy for you to cheat: at the end of each chapter, I've included some handy little bullet points that summarize the main stuff.

So by all means, read the whole thing if you'd like to — I have, after all, gone to all the trouble of filling this book up with words and things that may be of equal parts entertainment and practical use — but if that's not your thing and you just want to pick up enough so it looks like you have, then feel free to just skim the end bits.

Now, at this point I also need to declare that I don't have any girls myself. Not a single one. In fact, I have quite the opposite: two boys. If I was being completely honest, and that probably is the best thing at this stage, I'm really glad that I have boys. This isn't because I think boys are better than girls, or that I think boys are easier — they're not, they're just different — in truth it's just because we outnumber their mother, and so when it comes to the vote for which DVD to hire on a Friday night, chances are it won't be anything with fairies, or ponies, or Barbies. Unless of course it's a film about something which eats fairies, ponies, and Barbies, which would be pretty cool. In any case I'm very glad that I have boys, because I'd struggle watching girly movies.

I could do it, but I'd struggle.

So then, how can I understand the needs of dads when it comes to raising girls if I don't actually have girls myself? Well, primarily because I've spent a long time working with dads and daughters. Over the course of the past 20 or so years I've seen buckets of them. I've seen everything from princesses to evil she-demons. I've seen sweet girls and savage girls, and everything in between. One of the things I've learned along the way is that this whole 'gentler sex' thing is a complete load of bollocks. There might be sugar and spice in there, but from time to time you will also encounter things like napalm and spring-loaded bear traps as well. We'll get to this later on, but just for now you should know that, even though I've never raised any girls, I've spent more time than most with more families than most and I've learned a thing or two along the way about what matters and what doesn't when it comes to raising little human beings made of sugar and spice, and napalm, and even bear traps.

There's another thing you should bear in mind as we're going along as well, and this is something I always say in my books and talks, and also in my sessions with parents: this is all just what I think. It isn't inscribed in stone, and I don't necessarily claim to be right. It's just what I think. You need to weigh up what I'm saying for yourself and see if it fits you and your family. For goodness sake don't believe something just because you read it in a book. I've read lots of things in parenting books that are simply someone's wacky opinion dressed up as fact. Worse still, I've seen lots of books where people say things like 'the research shows that ...' and then go on to make some outrageously overstretched point based on this 'research' which is completely unjustified. I'll show you what I mean in a little more depth in Chapter 7.

I do talk about research in this book because I think science has some really important things to tell us about the world of girls, and I've put the sources I've used in the endnotes section at the back of the book so you can go check this stuff out for yourself if you want. No one ever does, of course, which is why people who write books can say almost anything with complete impunity. However, I have made every effort I can to give you an honest account of what the relevant research about girls says — but don't necessarily believe it just because I say.

A good measure of healthy scepticism is always warranted whenever anyone is telling you how you should raise your kids. It's not an exact science, and it's not black and white. Be *very* suspicious of *anyone* who tells you that it is.

My agenda, just by the bye, is pretty simple. I think parenting has become ridiculously complicated. I think we over-think it, we worry about things that don't really matter, and we all need to calm down a bit. I think kids are over-protected and over-managed, and we need to step back a bit and let them actually figure stuff out for themselves. When I was a kid, if I got bored my parents would simply tell me to go outside and play.

And, incredibly, I did.

Even more incredibly, I didn't lose an eye, feel neglected, suffer abandonment issues, get abducted by paedophiles, or become addicted to methamphetamines. I just went outside and played.

Nowadays, we hover about our kids as if they were made of glass. They're not, and the world is no more dangerous now than it was when we were children. In fact, if anything it's never been safer to be a child. Don't believe me? Well, we'll get to that in a little while, but just for now let me say that dirty old men aren't hanging from every tree branch waiting to snatch every child they see, and your daughters, and my sons, need to get out there in the world and live their lives just like we used to do when we were their age.

Don't over-think it, is my agenda, because the business of raising children is nowhere near as complicated and fragile as we've all been led to believe.

One final thing before we push on. If you've read *Mother Raising Sons*, then you're going to notice that there are some sections in this book which are also in that book. The reason for that isn't because I ran out of things to say, it's that some of that stuff is just as important for dad's raising daughters as it is for mothers raising sons. I couldn't leave it out of this one just because I've already talked about it in that one. Having said that, I wouldn't want you to get all irritated, thinking I'd tried to fill in pages by sneaking that material in. It's here because it really needs to be here.

Right, enough preamble — time to get on with the actual amble.

2

What dads want

When I wrote this chapter in *Mothers Raising Sons,* it was quite a bit longer. The reason for this is that mothers have a lot more wants than fathers when it comes to raising kids. This doesn't mean they love them any more than we do, it's just that mums tend to worry about a lot more stuff. We, on the other hand, have much simpler needs. We just want to live a quiet life without getting in trouble, and without anyone getting angry at us.

Sure fathers want their daughters, and their sons for that matter, to be healthy, happy, and successful, but mostly we want to stay out of trouble. This is why we simply acquiesce to many of our wives'/partners' demands over many of the routine domestic tasks, such as hanging up the bathmat. We don't hang it up because we think she's right, or because we think hanging it up is best, we hang it up simply because it's easier. It simply isn't worth the hassle involved in taking a stand over not hanging it up.

The amazing thing is that the women in our lives often don't understand that simple point. They think we do it because we're convinced of the inherent moral worth of hanging up bathmats.

Nope. It's simply not worth the hassle that *not* doing it would bring.

It's much the same way when it comes to children, and especially to daughters, and especially especially teenage daughters. We're going to spend a bit of time going over the whole teenage-daughter thing, because for most dads that's where things get tricky. The first stage is usually fairly straightforward, because most little girls think their dads are wonderful. It's the bit that comes after that which causes dads the most trouble.

First come the hormones, then come the dramas, then comes the almost overpowering urge to run. I suspect that many of the men who flee their old lives to join the French Foreign Legion are running away from difficult teenage daughters. This is a pretty drastic course of action. If you don't believe me, go YouTube 'Foreign Legion' and you'll see that — while it might sound romantic, and a little tempting if you have a really nasty case of teenage-daughter-itis — there are far less drastic ways to manage things.

The other thing that many dads of daughters want is to stop their daughters from hitching up with idiots. This might seem a bit paternalistic, but it's hard to be the Pater and not feel a little paternalistic. I think it would be fair to say that almost all dads have an inherent suspicion of boys, mostly for the blindingly obvious reason that we all used to be one, and so we know that underneath all the 'pleases' and 'thank yous' they are only interested in one thing.

No good.

No bloody good.

Worse still, she will eventually marry one of these boys, or end up living with him. Sometimes it's hard to know which is worse. We also know, from having been the boy, that fathers start to lose influence over their daughters' lives as the game progresses. One day she will listen more to him than to you, which begs the question how you can stop her from ending up with an idiot.

It's complicated, but it can be done.

So, basically, that's all dads want for their daughters in my opinion: we want them to be happy, healthy, and successful (however they choose to define that for themselves), and we don't want them ending up living with some idiot.

Is that too much to ask?

Tips on
What dads want

☆ We want our kids to be happy and healthy.

☆ We want large flat-screen televisions and the freedom to watch whatever interests us, and even the stuff that doesn't.

☆ Mostly, we just want to stay out of trouble.

☆ And we don't want our kids to end up with an idiot.

3

On girls, parenting books, 'parenting experts', and 'parenting experts' who write about girls in parenting books

Here's the dilemma I constantly face: I truly believe that a large part of the reason so many parents have lost confidence in themselves and in their judgement is because of all the bloody 'experts' telling us what to do. Too many bloody parenting books and too many bloody parenting shows on the telly. And yet I still find myself compelled to write books like this, and occasionally make parenting shows on the telly.

Hang on, you're thinking, *but if you write this stuff how can you say that parenting books are the problem?*

Easy. I just said it. Just then.

Well isn't that, you know . . . a bit bloody rich? You're complaining about too many parenting books and yet you're in the business of writing the damn things?

Tell me about it.

So why do you do it?

I'm basically pretty lazy.

What do you mean?

I'm lazy. I figured that there were really only two ways of telling ordinary mums and dads that, in my humble opinion, things have got a little mad. The first was to ring everyone up and have a chat to them on the phone, which would take a very long time and would also run into language problems. The other way was to write it all down in books and stick some of it on the telly. All round, that second option seemed like a far easier way of doing it.

But why do we need yet another parenting book?

We don't.

What?

We don't. Not really. The truth is that most people actually do a pretty good job of raising their kids. And most kids turn out OK in the end.

So why write more of them then?

Because, paradoxically, the best way to show people that they don't need experts telling them how to raise their children is to write a book telling them that. Plus there are plenty of wise parents I've spoken to over the years who've told me all sorts of interesting stuff, and it's nice to share some of that with everyone else.

So you're not telling people how to raise their daughters?

No, I'm not, except in the bits where I am. I'm also saying you shouldn't necessarily believe anything I say until you've tried it out for yourself to see whether what I say fits your situation. You're the only one raising your kids, so you need to question everything people tell you about what's good for your kids and what isn't. At best, all anyone is giving you is an opinion. Nothing more, nothing less. You need to decide for yourself how much weight you're going to give that opinion.

I also think it's important for me to outline exactly where I sit on the whole girl thing. That's important because I'm a guy writing a book about how to raise girls. The thing about parenting books is that there's always an underlying ideology, some world view that's either clear or hidden; either way, it informs the handy hints and suggestions the writers dole out. For example, if they think that girls are on the whole quite good but that there are still some things boys can do that girls can't, then they're going to spin things a certain way. They might be inclined to write a little more about how you should teach girls to be gentle and kind, and to fully express their innate motherly girliness. If they think that God made girls and boys a particular way and never the twain shall meet, they're also going to write a particular kind of book. Which is why, for the reasons I've just talked about, I think it's quite important for people to make their politics explicit.

I'm all for girls being gentle and kind, I see no real harm in that; but I've watched *Alien I* through *IV*, so I also think it's important for girls to be able to kick ass as much as the next guy. Ripley, aka Sigourney Weaver, didn't scream and sprain her ankle: she dealt to the big ugly alien nasty with a vengeance. Of course this doesn't mean that all girls literally have to kick ass like Ripley did, but I think girls have ass-kicking in them just as much as boys do, something we'll come back to in a little more detail in Chapter 18, 'The semi-myth of the gentler sex'. Female ass-kicking may not always get expressed in quite the same way as it does in boys, but I think it's there.

We hear a lot about the whole Mars and Venus stuff these days, and that's because it has a certain popular appeal. Men and women feel quite different, and so it's quite tempting to believe that we really are from different planets. Even if we put aside the ridiculous shoes that women wear, there's a whole bunch of other things as well. Surely this means our brains must be hardwired differently?

Not really.

I'll get into all this in a little bit, because it's quite important stuff to think about if you're raising girls, but for now let me say that I think girls really can do almost anything. They can't pee into the toilet standing up, but apart from that I think they can do everything else we can do, just as well as we can. If Barack Obama hadn't been so completely bloody cool, we probably would have had the first woman President of the United States. None of that is new to us here in New Zealand, though, because not only were we the first country in the world to give women the vote, but we also had a woman running the country for ages.

So in a nutshell, this is my position on the whole thing: girls might seem quite different, they might sound quite different, they might like different things, they might talk about those things in different ways, and as a general rule have trouble changing car tyres, but I think we're all far more alike than we are different. That's going to seem a little dumb at this stage, particularly given the previous chapter, but bear with me and we'll get back to this one a little further down the road.

Most of all I think our daughters can do anything our sons can do, including flying Apache Attack Helicopters, running multinational companies, cutting hair, building bridges, boxing, burning bras, transplanting kidneys, taking notes in meetings, running meetings, getting coffee, demanding coffee, arresting criminals, committing crimes, making babies, writing novels, juggling, digging ditches, singing songs, and banging gongs.

All these things, and much much more.

Tips on

Parenting books and 'parenting experts'

☆ All parenting books have some kind of agenda going on.

☆ Mine is that I think that parenting has all got a bit too complicated, and we take it all a bit too seriously.

☆ Most of all, it's important to remember that any parenting advice you get is just someone's opinion. Don't believe *anything* anyone tells you about how to raise your kids until you've tried it out for yourself first to see how it fits.

◊ Will people like her more if she's smart, or if she's beautiful?

◊ Is she strong? Is it OK to be strong?

◊ What kinds of things do girls do? What can't they do?

◊ Can she really do anything boys can do? Does she want to do any of those things anyway?

Once you start thinking about all the stuff your daughter is going to have to start to get her head around in the first decade of her life, it's pretty clear that you should be playing a fairly big role in helping her begin to sort through it all. The last thing you want to do is leave her to get her answers from all the popular-culture rubbish that's out there.

So it would be a mistake, in my opinion, to simply coast through the first bit just because it's appears easier than the next bit. The first bit is an important staging area for the second bit. I think it's crucial to see the first bit as the place where you lay the foundations of your relationship that will get you both through the second bit. If you mess up the first bit, then the second bit tends to be a lot harder.

It's a little like if Eisenhower had sat down with his generals on the morning of 5 June 1944 and said: 'I'm thinking it's about time we went over and kicked that little Nazi bastard's ass. How's tomorrow for you guys?' He didn't, because you can't simply start planning the Allied invasion of Europe the day before you invade. It's not something you chuck together at the last minute. That kind of thing takes a little planning, because there are all kinds of logistical issues that need to be addressed. The same can also be said for raising daughters. You can't just walk in at the last minute and expect that it's all going to go your way. Well, you can, but it probably won't work.

To help you out, here is my take on what I think are the top five tasks you might want to focus on during the first bit:

1 *Stake your claim early*
If you want to be part of her life later on, you need to be part of it from the beginning. I'm probably going to harp on a bit about this, and you might get sick of me saying it, but that's because it's so bloody important. It's not even hard: all you need to do is hang out with her.

2 *Build common interests*
The whole girl-thing can sometimes throw up a few natural blocks to father–daughter relationships, because we seem to be programmed to like different things. If you leave that to its own devices, chances are you'll end up without much in common. When she's little she'll be into pretty much whatever you're into, so you'd be wise to find something you can both do together when she gets older. It might be fishing, walking in the mountains, base jumping, whatever you can find that hooks you both.

3 *Be her go-to guy*
You want her to grow up thinking that you're the guy she comes to when she has problems. The way you do that is you make it obvious right from the start that you'll stop what you're doing and listen to her. Then you'll help her work out what to do. A lot of dads wait until it's too late for this. You can't suddenly expect to be her go-to guy when she's 13 if you've spent the past decade brushing her off. Her problems at five might seem a little trivial, but you need to remind yourself that they're practice for the much bigger problems which will arrive later on.

4 *Make sure she goes to sleep every night of her life knowing that you are on her side.*
Even if you've had a bad day, and even if she's been plonked in time-out, and even if she's been writing you little notes saying she doesn't want you as her dad anymore, make sure she always goes to sleep knowing that

you're her dad and that you're on her side. It's a simple little thing, but most of the really important things are in my experience.

5 *Have as much fun as you possibly can*
They are only little once, and it's important to remember this. She will be a little girl for a blink, and once that's gone you never get it back. Make sure you make all the time you can to just enjoy the heck out of this part of the ride. I've talked to many dads who wished they'd spent less time at work and more time with their kids — don't be one of those.

That last point is particularly important. They are only little once, and, even though sometimes it seems to drag, it will be over before you know it. You only get one go at her childhood, so make sure you're there for as much of it as you can, and have as much fun as you can.

A technical note on playing with girls

In a particularly revealing study, researchers examined mums' and dads' monitoring of their preschool children when they engaged in risky play. Specifically they watched the parents' behaviour as their kids completed two tasks: walking across a catwalk ladder that was 5 feet high, and walking across and dismounting from a beam that was 3 feet high. They found that fathers of daughters stood closer to their daughters than the fathers of sons, and followed them more closely as well. So it seems that there is some good evidence that dads tend to hover about their girls much more than they do their boys.

Here's the thing: if we're going to tell our girls they can do anything, we need to practise *showing* them that as well. Preschool girls are just as physically able to do these things as preschool boys. What you don't want to do is let some unconscious belief that she's more fragile than a boy elbow you into teaching her to be scared of the world. Self-confidence comes from achieving things, not from having your parents hovering about waiting to catch you all the time.

She might well bloody her knees, or even break an arm, but that stuff mends just as quickly in girls as it does in boys.

A further technical note on the sometimes tricky matter of physical affection and girls

When I was about to start writing this book, a man popped into my office one day. He was walking past, saw my name on the door, and decided to come in to ask if I'd sign a copy of one of my books for his wife. (I don't know why people only get the actual author to sign their books. I decided long ago to sign other people's books I'd bought on the authors' behalf, based on the notion that no one would ever know. So if you look on my bookshelf, you will see that Stephen King signed *The Stand* for me with the dedication: *For Nigel, one of my oldest and dearest friends. Best wishes, Stephen.* I also have a copy of Barack Obama's *The Audacity of Hope*, signed with the dedication: *Thanks, Nigel, I couldn't have done it without you. President Obama.* I am perhaps most proud of my copy of *Macbeth* which is dedicated thusly whence forth: *A rose by any other name is still a Nigel. William Shakespeare. PS: Thanks for your input around that double bubble bit which really had me buggered for a while.*)

As I was signing this man's book, I asked him about the kinds of issues he'd like to see in a book for dads of daughters. The very first thing that he said was that he'd like some idea about when it wasn't OK to cuddle his girls anymore.

'How old are they?' I asked.

'Seven and nine.'

'What do you want to know about all that, then?'

'Well, you know, you hear all this stuff about fathers being accused of molesting their daughters, so you don't want to do anything that could be taken the wrong way. Especially once they start to hit puberty and they probably start to feel a bit awkward as well.'

'So you want to know when's a good time to stop the physical affection?' I asked. I really liked this guy even though I'd only just met him. He was a great dad. I had no scientific basis on which to make that judgment, no evidence at all other than a gut feeling. Sometimes you just know.

He nodded. 'Yeah.'

'Never.'

He laughed, and it was a good sound. The sound of someone who knows he's doing the very thing he was put here on the ground to do. He was a dad.

'You *never* stop doing that stuff,' I said. 'You might need to pay a little closer attention to her signals when puberty kicks off, but if you're sensitive to all that then you'll know when to give her a cuddle and when to let her be. You *never* stop, though, because she'll *always* need it.'

'But what about all you hear about sexual abuse?'

'I've spent the past 20 years working with kids who've been sexually abused, and with the men who do it, and in all that time I have never once had a case where a good dad's honest intentions were misunderstood. Kids know whether something's OK or not. If you're doing a bad thing, they know. It might take them a while to be able to talk about it, but they know. The opposite is true, too: if you're a good dad giving your daughter a hug, she's going to know that.'

'But what about all those cases you see on telly?'

I shrugged. 'I'm not saying that doesn't happen. I've met dads who have been accused of doing things I don't believe they've done, but in every one of these cases it was in the middle of a nasty custody dispute where the only person the child ever allegedly disclosed anything to was the embittered ex-partner. Those cases are very rare, though, because when kids disclose someone's been doing bad stuff to them it's usually very clear who that person is and what they've been doing.'

'So I keep giving my girls hugs then?' he said.

I nodded. 'As many as you've got in you.'

'Phew,' he said, obviously relieved.

Phew indeed.

You have to wonder what the hell we've come to when good dads worry about when they should stop giving their daughters hugs. How did we all get to such a sorry state?

Phew in-bloody-deed.

Stage Two

everything that comes after the first stage

We're going to explore all this in quite a bit of detail over the rest of this book, particularly from Chapter 14 onwards. Some of the chapters that follow apply to both the first bit and the second bit, and some are about the second bit only. It's all pretty obvious, so I won't labour the point anymore.

Best just get on with it.

Tips on

Basic girl-ology

☆ The only developmental stages that really matter to dads are: the first stage, which is everything up until puberty starts to kick in; and the second stage, which is everything that comes next.

☆ Most dads find the first stage pretty straightforward.

☆ Don't underestimate the importance of the first stage, though, just because it's easier. This is where you lay the groundwork that will get you both through the second stage.

☆ How you do that is by:
  — staking your claim early
  — building common interests
  — being her go-to guy
  — making sure she goes to sleep every night of her life knowing that you are on her side
  — having as much fun as you possibly can.

☆ It's just as important to play rough with girls as it is with boys, and to let them take risks.

☆ Physical affection is important no matter what age she is.

5

Girl-talk: communicating with the other side

The best example I think you can get of how men and women talk differently is how we talk about telephone calls from our in-laws. If she is on the phone to her parents, the call usually lasts far longer than your call to your parents; but the real difference becomes clear afterwards. Men usually ask something along the line of 'How are your folks?'

When we ask this, what we really want to know is just the important fundamentals: Are they all still alive, and is everyone basically OK? What women interpret this as is a request for a verbatim transcript of the entire conversation. Distressingly, often women also want to give this word-by-word run-through of the conversation in the middle of the television programme we're currently watching. This is because they think we care more about our in-laws than we do about whatever is on telly at that moment. We sort-of do, usually, but right at that moment we're more interested in the telly.

Wouldn't it be fantastic if they got off the phone and just said: 'Yes they're both still alive, and generally things are going fine.'

In all honesty, what else would you want to know?

The same is also true in reverse, because when we get off the phone she asks: 'How's your mum?'

'Fine.'

'What's happening with your folks?'

'Uh . . . I dunno. Just the usual.'

'What did she say?'

Shrugs: 'She's fine; Dad's fine.'

'You must have talked about more than that — you were on the phone for 20 minutes.'

'Well . . . you know . . . we did, but basically everyone's fine.'

She frowns, and at this point you need to tread carefully, because you're knocking on the front door of an argument right there and then, so you need to keep your wits about you.

Why are men and women so different in how we talk about things? Well, we'll look at some of this in the later chapters on personality stuff and brain stuff, but really what this is about is the different cultures that men and women exist in. I don't think we're from Mars and Venus, respectively, but I do think men and women have some fundamentally different ways of getting their communication needs met. It's not about right or wrong ways to communicate — it's about being aware of the fact that we sometimes do it in fairly different ways.

Gathering intel

When men communicate, we almost always do it with a specific outcome in mind; but when women communicate, the outcome is often communication itself. When we're at work, I think men and women are both fairly equally outcome-focused; but in our personal relationships with our loved ones and our friends, we do talk differently.

So what does all this mean when you're the father of a girl? Does this mean you have to learn to talk like a girl? Do you have to sit down with plastic teacups and discuss fairies and ponies? Do you need to listen to endless diatribes about who said and did what to whom at school that day?

Sometimes, no; sometimes, yes.

The great advantage that you have as the father of girls is that talking about stuff often comes much easier to girls than it does for boys. With boys it's all about trying to coax information out of them most of the time, but with girls it's quite the opposite.

As one concrete example of this, my own son, who's nine at time of writing, keeps the details of his day pretty close to his chest. If I ask how school was, he'll mostly say 'fine'. If I ask him what he did, he might tell me about one or two things, but that's about it. In truth I think the school could burn to the ground and he'd still say 'fine' when I asked him how his day was.

Compare that with the answer I get when I ask the same question to one of his best friends, a girl in his class. She's great. All you need to do is ask how school is going, and we find out every little thing that's happened since the last time we asked her that question. It's pretty much the best way we have of keeping up with the latest news. She not only knows how other people are doing, but she also knows whose parents are separated, who lives with what parents, and often some of the background life history of different kids' parents as well.

How she can know all this at age nine is a testament to the natural inclination girls seem to have to gather social intelligence. I'm firmly convinced that the best spies we could possibly have would be nine-year-old girls. Just air-drop them into the local school and you'll have a line into any information you need. I guarantee that my son's little friend would've been able to able to get the Soviet launch codes in under a week.

The Big Three

Often people make the simple act of communicating with another human being look like it's something just short of rocket science. There are books and books on communication. Some of them are useful; some of them are a little silly. Sometimes the only way to say something is to say something.

I don't think communication is rocket science, unless of course it's between two scientists talking about jet propulsion systems, in which case clearly it would be. For the rest of us, though, it's just talking about stuff.

Nothing more, nothing less.

So this is my dad's guide to girl-talk cut down into three simple little points. Nothing complicated here, and no special words or phrases to remember.

1 *Make the effort*
   I cannot stress enough the importance of making the effort. You don't have to do anything in particular; you simply need to do something. Communication won't happen by itself: it needs at least two people to be involved. If you put the effort in and make sure that your daughter knows you are interested in her, then even if you don't always say the right thing you'll still be giving her the one thing she needs the most: your time.

2 *Don't try to solve the problem all the time*
   It's worth remembering that girls don't always want you to solve the problem; sometimes, they just want to talk about how they feel. This can be hard for us, because being practical creatures we want to fix the problem. Oddly, though, girls sometimes just want to *talk* about the problem rather than fix it. You should solve the problem some of the time, for sure, because she will want that from you, but don't do it *all* the time. Sometimes she simply wants to tell someone how she's feeling.

3 *Ask questions*
   The great thing about questions is that they do more than simply gather information — they also build links between fathers and daughters. If you're asking her questions, you're showing her you're interested, and that is a very

good thing. Again, practical creatures that we are, most men prefer to ask only enough questions to allow them to understand the problem, and then proceed to make a series of statements about how to fix the problem. Splash the question around a bit — they like that stuff.

And that's it: simple as one, two, three.

Oh sure, I could make it a lot more complicated than that, but I really don't think the world needs any more spin. I think there's more than enough rubbish floating about already. You don't have to talk like a girl, but you do need to talk *with* your girl, and mostly that's going to involve simply listening to her. The more you do, the better she will feel about herself, and the more able she will be to deal with the myriad trials that life will throw at her.

The father who temporarily lost his mind, voice, and daughter

I'd been talking with the Bartlett family for about 10 minutes and found I could go no further without pointing out the rather large pachyderm sitting in the corner. Mrs Bartlett was a lawyer, Mr Bartlett was an accountant, and Sally was 14 and awful. She wasn't permanently awful, however; she was just 'situationally awful'. Up until 11 she'd been nice, but it had all gone a bit downhill from there. She wasn't killing kittens or robbing banks, though; she was just permanently put-out and affronted. Her parents had brought her along because they were worried that she seemed to be so grumpy with them all the time.

That wasn't the elephant, though. No, the real elephant in the room was the fact that Mr Bartlett hardly spoke. In fact he pretty much did the opposite of speaking, which was emanating a kind of despairing silence while his wife and daughter hammered it out.

'Um, hang on a wee minute', I said. 'I need to ask something before we go on.' Everyone looked at me — well, almost everyone. Sally simply rolled her eyes and looked at some point above my desk that clearly she found annoying. 'How come you aren't saying anything?' I asked Mr Bartlett.

He shuffled in his seat and looked a bit uncomfortable, as if he wasn't accustomed to being part of all this. 'I've found it's best to say as little as possible around Sally, because I usually say the wrong thing.'

'The wrong thing?' I asked. 'What would that be?'

'Honestly? I don't know, because it seems like everything I say is the wrong thing.'

I looked over at Sally, who, bless her, looked utterly affronted and put-out and generally snippy all in the one pained expression. 'I wouldn't think it's very hard to offend her,' I said. 'She seems to have quite the gift for taking offence.'

She gave me a single baleful glare and looked away.

'Wow,' I said, 'that was very good. You could kill flies with a glare like that. You're like an organic insecticide. You could wipe them out with a single glare and, what's more, the glare is completely biodegradable and carbon neutral.'

Dad laughed.

Sally didn't.

'So, you seriously don't say anything around her?'

'Obviously, I don't say absolutely nothing, but I try and keep my communication to a minimum.'

'Why? Because you're worried about saying the wrong thing?'

He nodded.

I understood it completely. He was like a soldier in World War I who flatly refused to leave the trenches and walk towards the German lines, on the very reasonable basis that everyone who did that was mown down by German machine guns.

'You're like a soldier in World War I who refuses to leave the trenches and charge the Germans, on the very reasonable basis that you'll get mown down by their machine guns,' I said.

He laughed. 'I supposed I am.'

'The only mistake you're making is that the Germans used actual bullets — but she's just bluffing. She's firing blanks and hoping that everyone's going to be so scared and confused they won't notice.'

Sally looked at me and sneered again.

'See,' I said to her dad, pointing out the lack of blood and entrails spread all over the chair, 'blanks. She just gave me a baleful glare and it didn't leave a scratch.'

'I'd never thought of it like that,' he said.

'Don't worry about saying the right thing. There's no such thing as the right thing. Just say anything and see what happens next. If you let her bluff you into silence, then you'll all be living in the trenches for years. Get up there on the parapet and do the jig. You need to engage the enemy in a witty exchange of pleasantries, or even unpleasantries for that matter. Whatever you do, don't let a few blank rounds trick you into keeping your head down. She needs you to lead the way, not back away.'

He thought for a few moments, and then looked over at his daughter. 'Is that true?' he asked her.

'No,' she snarled.

He looked back at me, and I gave him a visual nudge.

'Well, I think it is,' he said. 'I think I'm going to say what I think from now on, and you're going to have to learn to live with it.'

She sighed, much as one sighs when a particularly stupid and offensive person sits next to one, and slumped down in her chair.

'I think you need to think more about how you speak to your mum,' he said.

And just like that, the elephant stood up, adjusted his braces, and ambled out of the room.

Tips on
Girl-talk

☆ Make the effort.

☆ Don't try to solve the problem all the time.

☆ Ask lots of questions.

6

The girl crisis — sadly you missed it, you were too late

I don't know what it is about us humans, but we do seem to love a good crisis. At the time of writing, it's the so-called swine flu, but that one already seems to be fizzling out. I started off taking the whole swine flu thing seriously, mostly because it's hard not to when CNN is bringing you live updates from the World Health Organization every half-hour. After a while, though, it seemed fairly clear that this was a practice for the oft-talked-about but never-quite-materializing 'Big One', rather than actually *being* the Big One.

If I was being really honest, I would have to say I was a little disappointed. Many years ago I'd read Stephen King's plague novel, *The Stand*, and I was rather looking forward to the 'super flu' emptying the place out a bit. Sure, it would be kind of sad to lose most of the human race, but the thought of finally getting some peace and quiet and a little 'me time' kind of appealed.

So even though there was a pandemic, it seemed a little limp.

Interestingly, when I was a kid I remember one of the big issues was African Killer Bees. Apparently they were coming, and they were angry little sods. Your average bee is pretty placid, but your African Killer Bee is pretty much the complete opposite of placid. You piss off an African Killer Bee and you are going to find yourself in a world of hurt. Personally, I blame whoever named them in the first place. If I'd grown up with a name like 'African Killer Nigel', I'd probably feel like I had something to prove as well.

In any case, the swarms of angry killer bees never turned up; I don't know where they went. Most likely they flew off to wherever it is old crises go when we get bored with them. It didn't matter, because along the way we've also had the Ebola virus, AIDS, Communism, nuclear armageddon, and George W Bush. All of these things were a crisis in their own way, but one by one they all fizzled out.

Phew.

The same can be said for the 'girl crisis'. It's lost a lot of steam over the past few years, because girls have actually been doing pretty well in all kinds of areas. So well in fact that it prompted a bit of a 'boy crisis' movement, with many people writing influential books on the causes behind the boy crisis and its likely impact. I've written about that elsewhere, but basically my take on the boy crisis, after having looked at a lot of the research and statistics for myself, is that it's exaggerated. Some boys are in crisis, but then some boys have always been in crisis. I'd place myself squarely in the camp of people who believe that really it's not so much about boys doing worse, as much as it is about girls doing better.

What is pretty obvious, when you look at the big picture of what the international research is telling us, is that boys and girls on the whole tend to have different problems. For girls, the issues seem to be more about depression, suicidal thinking and attempts, and eating disorders. Girls are also less likely to achieve at the highest levels in mathematics and science — but before you go writing off your daughter's career as a mathematician, wait until we come back to this in the next chapter, because the maths/science thing is not as straightforward as it seems at first glance.

Reading the above can be a little alarming: the thought that the issues your daughter is most likely to face are depression, wanting to kill herself, and eating disorders is likely to raise your anxiety levels just a little. The reality is that all of these statistics and numbers are essentially meaningless at the individual level. My intention in talking about these issues here is not to scare; in fact it's the opposite, because what I'd really like to do is give you a way to put these kind of doom-and-gloom statistics and proclamations into context.

I wouldn't want you to think that I'm knocking crises entirely, because such information does serve a useful purpose. For girls, the 1990s marked a pretty belated entry into the field of public interest. As is often the case, it took a book to get the public and the media's attention, and for girls that book was *Reviving Ophelia,* written by Mary Pipher and published in 1994. This was a *New York Times* bestseller for years, and not just because of the fact that Pipher has a singularly engaging turn of phrase. Pipher's main thrust was that girls were growing up in a 'girl poisoning culture' and she talked about the kinds of things that were always going to get people's attention: 'body mutilating diets', self-cutting, rebelling against parents, drugs, alcohol, and unprotected sex.

It was grim and frightening stuff, but in some ways it had to be in order to get people's attention, because up until then girls had been pretty much left out of things when it came to the public and academic debate. In the 1970s, for example, there were a lot of people studying and writing about 'youth culture', but the majority of this stuff was about male youth culture with girls either being left out or added on as an afterthought.

All that started to change after *Reviving Ophelia.* Suddenly, everyone started to get concerned about their daughters, and, just like rap music, the wave started in the United States and spread throughout the rest of the developed world. Soon we were worried about all kinds of things to do with our girls. The good thing about all this was that the politicians sat up and took notice, and before you knew it there were all kinds of programmes and initiatives aimed at helping girls.

And so, not surprisingly, things started to get better.

Now, that notwithstanding, you are still going to come across some pretty dire-sounding statistics from time to time. The reason for that is that scary shit helps to sell books, and it gets you a larger, more attentive audience. If I'd called this book *The Three Things Most Likely to Kill Our Daughters and/or Drive Them Insane*, I would undoubtedly sell a lot more copies. I didn't call it that because I don't like that stuff, and, even though the extra cash would be nice, I don't think it's helpful to go around scaring people into buying whatever it is you're selling.

So let's take just one example of doom-and-gloom statistics, and think about what it might mean in the real world. Let's take the completely fictitious statistic that girls are 67% more likely to be eaten by sharks than boys. Obviously this is isn't true, and I wouldn't want to offend any sharks by giving the impression that they preferred eating girls over boys. So far as I'm aware, sharks are pretty much equal-opportunity carnivores, and, even though they don't eat people all that much, when they do I'm sure they would eat just about anyone regardless of creed, colour or sex. I'm sure sharks would even eat Nazis if the occasion arose, although from all that I've seen of Nazis they don't seem to hang out on the beach much. I have never, for instance, seen Nazis playing volleyball at the beach, or paddling with their little Nazi children. Despite this, I'm sure that, given the choice between, say, a Nazi and a member of Amnesty International, the shark would simply eat whoever was closest and/or fattest.

They just don't care much about political affiliations.

All that aside, how might you understand the statistic that says your daughter is 67% more likely to be eaten by a shark than your son?

I'd suggest that you pretty much ignore it.

Seriously?

Yup.

But isn't that statistic too alarming to ignore?

Not really.

Why not?

Because it's talking about averages for the population of girls as a whole; it's not really telling you anything meaningful about your own daughter. Some girls will have no risk at all of being eaten by sharks, and some will have a very high risk.

So how can you tell which one your girl is?

The thing with any dire statistic is that if your kids really are in trouble then it's usually pretty bloody obvious.

Yeah, but how do you know?

Well, we'll talk about some of the specifics — like sex, drugs, and self-harm — later, but really all you need to do is pay attention. If your daughter lives hundreds of miles from the sea, then she is at almost no risk of being eaten by sharks. On the other hand if she lives in the sea, in a house made from rotting fish guts, and spends her days spooning fresh animal blood into the water, her chances are much higher.

You're saying that the big numbers don't matter — all that really matters is what your daughter is doing?

That's exactly what I'm saying: pay attention to what's in front of you, not what's on the news. Statistics are interesting, but they're simply describing a population in general terms. They don't *prescribe* what will happen to our daughters. What actually happens is down to them, and down to us.

So how do we minimize the risk of some of the bad things you hear about in the media?

That's what the rest of this book is all about — which is how to do the best job you can to raise a confident, independent girl who knows who she is, and what she wants, and isn't afraid to stand up for that.

Yeah, yeah, but how do we do that?

Probably a good start would be to tell her that if she does go swimming in the sea, to make sure she doesn't pee in her wetsuit, swim with dogs, swim at dusk, or swim whilst towing a bag of fresh blood. That's going to give her a head start on the shark issue, and we'll cover the rest as we go along.

Tips on
The girl crisis

☆ You missed it by about 15 years.

☆ The good news is that girls are generally doing OK.

☆ Phew.

7

Mars, Venus, and sexual pseudoscience

Mars and Venus are, without doubt, very different. Mars, for instance, is 133.3 million miles from the sun, whilst Venus is a scant 67.48 million miles. Mars is smaller than Venus whose radius is 2,654 kilometres larger. Mars also has a smidgeon less carbon dioxide and nitrogen in its atmosphere (1.2% and 0.8%, respectively), but has a whopping 1.593% more argon, which, if you like argon, can only be a good thing. I'm fairly neutral so far as argon is concerned myself, but I'm sure there must be life forms somewhere out there in the infinite vastness of space which think argon is pretty neat. Mars also has two moons, compared with Venus's none, but is on average quite cold (-4°C) compared with Venus which is really quite toasty (460°C).

So I'd completely agree with the premise that Mars and Venus are quite different — the *real* Mars and Venus, that is, but not the Mars and Venus used in metaphorical form to refer to men and women. It's a nice metaphor, and it has certainly made John Gray — of *Men Are from Mars, Women Are from Venus* fame — an awful lot of money. It just isn't supported by the actual science of sex differences between the brains. Simply because something sounds cool, doesn't mean it's necessarily true.

And there have been some very cool-sounding, but completely outlandish claims made about the 'female brain' over the past few years. Here's just a sampling of them:

◊ Girls have more sensitive hearing than boys, which is why girls often complain that their father is yelling at them when he thinks he's speaking normally.

◊ Girls' visual systems are hardwired completely differently to those of boys, which is why girls draw different kinds of pictures and use more colours.

◊ Girls are able to talk about their feelings better than boys, because these two different parts of their brains are more connected than boys' brains from a much earlier age.

◊ Girls tend to be more empathetic, whereas boys only seem to notice something is amiss when someone cries or threatens to hurt them.

◊ Girls talk more than boys.

◊ Girls are better at English, and boys are better at maths.

Like I said, it looks great, and it sounds great, but the actual scientific basis of all this is anything but great. Of course that hasn't stopped a lot of people making a lot of money writing books which ooze 'sexual pseudoscience'. This term isn't mine, in fact I first came across it while I was researching my book on boys on a website called *The Language Log*. Professor Mark Liberman, a contributor to this website, has written extensively on this subject, and in particular on the matter of boys and girls, and their respective brains. I would strongly suggest that you spend a little time having a look at this for yourself. I'm going to spend some time describing some of the major critiques here, but don't just take my word for it — go have a look for yourself.

You might be thinking at this point that knowing about all this science isn't that important — but, trust me, it is.

Why?

Because you need to know how shonky some of this stuff is so that you don't get sucked in by all the hype.

What do you mean?

Well, take this little corker from *The Washington Times*:

> Recent studies using MRI scans show clearly that the average boy's brain develops much more slowly than the average girl's. Some studies show that the brain of a 17-year-old boy looks like the brain of a 13-year-old girl. The men don't catch up with the women until about age 30.

Or how about this rather compelling piece of information about how girls respond to stress?

> The girl brain circuits are arranged and fuelled by oestrogen to respond to stress with nurturant activities and the creation of protective social networks.

I mean, *sheesh*, our brains don't catch up with girl brains until we're 30? And a 17-year-old boy's brain looks like a 13-year-old girl's brain? And all that stuff about how girls' brains are fuelled by hormones to get all nurturing when they're stressed, and then get together for girl-talk — what's all that about? Is it really true?

We'll get to that in just a lickity-split, but for now I'm sure you can see how that kind of information is going to have a serious impact on the thinking of what we do with our daughters and our sons. All this information and more is being thrown around by all kinds of people in all kinds of places. Some of it is on the internet — on the great, wild, untamed wilderness of parenting message boards — but some of it is being thrown around in conferences, in policy meetings with important people, and in staffrooms in our schools.

The problem is that we find neuroscience so gosh-darned

convincing. All you need to do is sprinkle a few pictures of brain scans somewhere in the argument and you can convince the vast majority of people that what you're saying is gold, when really it's just very shiny snake oil. To their credit, the neuroscientists are a little worried about all this themselves, and have even done research which shows that people are far more likely to believe a poor explanation for a psychological phenomenon if it contains some kind of neuroscientific information even where that information is irrelevant to the logic of the explanation. So even though the neuroscience has no logical relevance to what is being explained, the mere *presence* of it makes subjects feel like it is a better explanation.

This next section is crucial to understanding pseudoscience, how it works, and how silly it is. This material is so important to understanding the context of current parenting debates that I also set it out in my book *Mothers Raising Sons*. I'm doing it again here because I think it's stuff we all need to know about. Because of that, what I'm going to do is give you a crash course in sexual pseudoscience, and try to inject a little reality into the reams and reams of ideology that so often surround the world of kids and brains, and particularly gender and brains. I would strongly suggest that you don't just believe my take on it: I've put the sources for all this material in the endnotes, and wherever possible I've provided links from the internet so you can find this research for yourself. Where that isn't possible, I've given the references for the scientific papers themselves, so if you want to you can check it out for yourself. Most readers won't, though, because few of us want to read a book and then have to go do a whole bunch of research to see if what we're being told is accurate. Instead, we assume that if someone says it in a book, then it must be something they've researched for themselves and are representing accurately. I mean you'd have to, right? Because if you said that something in a book was based on research and it wasn't, you'd get caught out, right? Surely the science police would get you? Surely you couldn't sell millions of copies of a book if you were making scientific claims that weren't backed up by the science you were quoting?

Surely you're not allowed to do that?

Right?

Mostly when people talk about brain scans they are talking about an fMRI, or functional Magnetic Resonance Imaging. There are all kinds of ways that scientists study the brain (here we go alphabet crazy: PET, EEG, sMRI, MRS, and DTI), but because fMRI is one of the most commonly used techniques I thought I'd give you a quick rundown of the issues with this technique alone, so you can get your head around how difficult this stuff is.

How fMRI works is that you put a given person inside a really big, really expensive machine, and it clicks and whirs and bangs for a bit. The end result of all the clicking, whirring and banging is that a computer produces an image of what is happening in that person's brain.

Except here's the complex bit (although let's be honest, the whole bloody thing seems pretty complex to most of us): it doesn't take a picture of neurons (brain cells) firing; instead, it measures brain activity indirectly by getting an electronic measure of changes in blood oxygenation called a BOLD (blood oxygenation level-dependent) signal. The rationale is that the more the brain cells are firing, the more blood oxygenation will change. The fMRI then turns these activation signals into 'voxels', small 3D cubes ($<3mm^3$) which are like the pixels on your digital camera.

So whilst it doesn't measure brain cell activity directly, the fMRI does it in a sneakily indirect way by measuring the BOLD signal, the stuff that changes as brain cells are firing, and turning that into the fMRI equivalent of a pixel, which for reasons we don't need to know about they call a voxel. The more the brain cells fire, the more the blood oxygenation will change, and so the stronger the activation signal will be, and the stronger the voxel on the final image will be.

That's pretty clever.

Yes, indeedy.

So what this means is that now we are able to make all kinds of statements about how people's brains work because we can get them to do stuff and then look at our nice little voxel-based picture of the brain?

Well, no, not really.

Oh.

Yeah.

So how come it isn't that simple?

It turns out, sadly, that there are a number of problems with making definitive statements based on fMRI pictures of the brain. It isn't just as simple as measuring the BOLD signals through a pretty pattern of voxels in a part of the fMRI scan which then tells us exactly how brains work.

Bummer.

Yeah, it's a bummer alright.

Is there a simple, not quite so drawn-out way of explaining why that is?

Sure there is: bullet points. Let me give you the fundamentals of why we need to be very careful in deciding what fMRI images (commonly called 'brain scans' in the media) are actually telling us:

◇ The most basic problem is that you can't test abilities in real-world settings. People are tested while they're lying inside a machine, so that's going to create problems generalizing back to actual abilities in the real world.

◇ The BOLD signal can change, based on the part of the brain being examined, the type of task or stimulus being used, the age and health of the person being scanned, and whether or not they've had caffeine or nicotine (although you'd hope that this last factor wouldn't be a common issue with kids). Basically, it's pretty variable.

◇ On top of all that, BOLD signals may also be different in the same person at different times, making it hard to establish a 'baseline'.

◇ Sometimes the part of the brain that is of interest may be too small for the pattern of voxels to stand out. Scientists are currently working on fMRIs that will be able to get the voxel down to 1mm³, which will greatly help, but we aren't there yet.

◇ We still don't know how BOLD signals are influenced by developing areas of the brain in children. Some studies have shown that there are similarities between the BOLD signals of children and adults, but there are still a lot of things that need to be worked out before we can make any definitive statements about what fMRI scans of children really mean.

◇ The statistics used to analyse the results are really complicated. There are lots of examples in the research literature where arguments break out because one group of researchers say that another group of researchers haven't got the maths right and so their results aren't what they thought they were.

The big message in all of this for all of us is that the 'brain scan' stuff we hear so much about isn't as cut-and-dried as it's sometimes painted to be. There are more claims about what fMRIs have 'proven' than I've had hot dinners, and there will no doubt be many more to come. I'm not saying it's all rubbish, because a machine that costs something in the vicinity of $3 million has to be doing something pretty clever; what I *am* saying is that we need to be a little cautious before we leap to a whole bunch of assumptions about what these images are telling us about ourselves, and particularly about our daughters.

Perhaps it's best to let an actual scientist, Dr John T Bruer (and admittedly he's written extensively about his scepticism regarding the claims often made about the implications of neuroscience for the real world), sum this one up:

If neuroscientists are to prevent their work from being misrepresented, they must think more critically about how their research is presented to educators and the public, and in particular they must be very cautious about even the most innocent speculation about the practical significance of basic research. They should remind the interested public that we are just at the beginning of our scientific inquiry into how neural structures implement mental functions and how mental functions guide behavior.

The thing about fMRI-based research, if you were to boil it right down to fat and bone, is that unless you're very rigorous in how you design, run, analyse, interpret, and talk about your study, there's a pretty big risk that anything you say may be partly, if not sometimes completely, bollocks.

Right, now that we're armed with a slightly better understanding of some of the limitations of the 'brain scan' science, and that we're more aware of how unreasonably persuasive even just the mention of neuroscience is, let's go back and have a look at some of those rather bold claims.

'Girls have more sensitive hearing than boys.'

This is an important claim, because in the past it has been used as a significant biological justification for single-sex schools. We'll look at the single-sex versus co-ed arguments as it relates to girls in Chapter 10, but just for now let's look at the claim itself. Some authors have claimed that if a 43-year-old man speaks to his 17-year-old daughter in what he thinks is a normal voice, she will hear it 10 times more loudly than he would.

Holy eardrums, Batman, that's quite a difference!

What's more, if this were true, it would have significant implications for how we talk to our daughters, and how we treat them at school as well. The line of logic here is that, because research has shown that girls' hearing is far more sensitive than that of boys, girls will do better in classes where the teachers speak softly (ie, lady teachers) whereas boys will do better where the teachers speak in loud voices (ie, the gentleman teachers).

So how much of that is actually true?

Well, it turns out that academics have traded blows on this one at length. If you want to see the whole argument on this matter laid out, you will find a link to a rather complex, but very interesting, analysis of the issue at the back of this book. If that kind of thing is your kind of thing, I'd encourage you to have a look at the article. I love that kind of stuff myself, but I know that not everyone does, so let me summarize how I see the matter evening out when one goes back and looks at the actual research on hearing differences between boys and girls, and the competing claims that are made about these differences.

Essentially, there are no meaningful differences between the hearing of boys and girls.

No meaningful differences?

Nope.

So where does that claim come from?

That's a good question, because, when I looked at the research which was being used to justify these somewhat extravagant claims of hearing differences, it seems pretty clear that the real picture is that there are small average differences between male and female hearing, with lots of overlap. This means that, while as a whole there is a difference in the *average* hearing sensitivity of girls and boys, there are lots of girls and lots of boys who are both higher and lower than the respective averages.

Small average differences, with lots of overlap: that's an important phrase, and you'll need to remember it because it's going to crop up again and again as we go along. Just for now, though, if anyone ever tells you that there are big differences in the sensitivity of boys' and girls' hearing, remember that actually there isn't.

'Girls' and boys' visual systems are hardwired completely differently.'

Why do girls tend to draw pictures with lots of bright colours, flowers, houses, and clouds, while boys draw pictures of monsters with guns for arms, shooting at guns with guns for arms, riding on tanks while throwing gun-shaped spears?

This is an interesting question, because if you go into any classroom you can fairly easily see that there is often a marked difference between the art that girls produce and the art that boys produce. To explain this, some writers and commentators have turned to our old friend neuroscience and come up with some fairly compelling stuff.

First, let me tell you the bit that's actually true.

It turns out that there *are* differences between male and female retinas. Microscopic studies of retinal cellular anatomy have shown that female retinas are thinner because they contain more of the smaller 'P ganglion cells', which are specialized to detect edges and colour, whereas male retinas are thicker because they contain the larger 'M ganglion cells', which are specialized to detect motion and depth.

As it turns out, this nicely explains why boys and girls draw different pictures. Girls have eyes that are hardwired to draw what they actually see, lots of stuff with lots of colours. Boys, on the other hand, have eyes that are hardwired to draw what their eyes see, which are basically action scenes without much colour. We're told that these differences between the hardwiring of boys and girls are big, and very important.

Very cool.

Except, of course, there is one quite important piece that's been left out, which is that this research is talking about the microanatomy of rat retinas.

Rats? You mean rats, as in the small, nocturnal rodents?

That's right: rats.

Isn't that . . . you know . . . a bit crap?

It is, as you say, a bit crap.

So have they looked at human children's retinas?

They have. And would it surprise you to learn that there are very small average differences, with lots and lots of overlap?

Not really.

It seems that, once again, we see that the science that these people are quoting doesn't actually support their argument. There are differences in the average thicknesses of male and female human retinas, but it's a very small difference (somewhere in the order of 3%), and there are a lot of individual differences between the girls and boys. So whatever the reason for the differences in girls' and boys' pictures, it doesn't seem like it has anything much to do with hardwired differences in their eyes.

'Girls are able to talk about their feelings better than boys, because these two different parts of their brains are more connected than boys' brains from a much earlier age.'

See, now that right there is A-grade prime-beef pseudo-neuro-sexo-nonsensico. As with all this stuff it sounds fantastic, and it's got just enough science in it to make it look like something Albert Einstein would have carved into the toilet wall in the men's room at the Instituta von Scientifica Studienschaft. It's like the closest thing to a dirty limerick that a great scientific mind such as his probably got.

One of the reasons it seems so scientifically nifty is that, as a general rule, girls do seem to talk about their feelings more than blokes do, and so all you have to do is throw in a little neuroscience and you've got something that will be regurgitated by journalists and 'parenting experts' *ad infinitum*.

Hopefully by now, though, you're starting to get a little bit of a 'yeah, right' response when you read stuff like this. So what's the real deal? Well, this statement — and variations on it — tend to flow back to a study done in 2001 on a grand total of 19 children aged from 9 to 17 years. What the researchers were looking at was essentially the level of communication between two important parts of the brain: the prefrontal cortex and the amygdala. The reason they were looking at these two parts of the brain is that the amygdala is a key part of the brain for essentially 'producing' emotions, and the prefrontal cortex is where we organize and interpret the information which comes from the amygdala. It's a little like the amygdala and the prefrontal cortex have a conversation to decide what we're feeling and why that is.

Effectively, and somewhat crudely put, if those two bits of your brain aren't talking to each other about what you're feeling, then you can't tell me what you're feeling or why. In reality it's far more subtle than that, but that's effectively the line of logic put forward by the sexual pseudoscience buffs.

What the original study reported was that there seemed to be a statistically significant difference between the development of these connections between girls and boys. The good news for you, as the father of daughters, is that girls seemed to develop much better connections between these two parts of their brain much earlier than the boys did. The only problem — although, actually, there were quite a few problems as you're welcome to go see for yourself, but I'll simply talk about this one — was that the study was based on the results of 19 children. In scientific terms that's an almost ridiculously small number, and so raises huge issues about how valid these results are to the wider population of all girls and all boys. In fact, the study's authors specifically said this in the peer-reviewed scientific paper, but it still didn't stop all kinds of people from making all kinds of bold, ridiculously over-stretched statements about what this all means.

'Girls talk more than boys.'

You would think that this one at least would be true. Surely this one has to be true? Most of us menfolk labour under the assumption that women talk more than we do. It's the subject of many a sitcom scene, and many a rolled eye between husbands, and fathers, too.

Girls just seem to talk a lot more than we do.

Except they don't.

You can't be serious.

Actually, I am. Once you put aside all the hoo-hah and try to find some actual science on this assertion, it quickly becomes apparent that there isn't very much. Having said that, there was one study done by Dr Matthias Mehl, a psychologist at the University of Arizona, who gave 400 men and women a voice-activated tape recorder and then counted the number of words that each person used in the course of a day.

And what did he find?

They talked about the same amount.

You're kidding?

I kid you not.

Do you mean 'about the same, but women talked a bit more'? Or about the same?

I mean about the same. There was a lot of variation within the men and the women groupings; some talked a lot more and some talked a lot less, but on average they talked about the same. So far as I know, no one has done any research looking at how much children talk, but my guess is that you'd find it's about the same then, too.

What about teenagers, though? Surely girls talk a lot more than boys then?

Maybe, but I'd also be willing to guess that if you gave a bunch of teenagers voice-activated tape recorders you'd probably find that boys talked a lot less to their parents than girls, but I still think they'd end up speaking about the same to each other, and to girls as well. Still, I hasten to point out that no one has actually done that so far as I'm aware — that's just my guess.

'Girls are better at English, boys are better at maths.'

There is good news here in abundance for the fathers of girls, because there is clear evidence that girls have been doing better and better in school, and many of the gaps that used to exist between boys and girls have now closed up. Indeed, several large studies have been done which show that girls have closed the maths gap. In fact, girls have closed all kinds of gaps and are taking to the whole school thing with quite some gusto. It seems that many of the historical gender differences we've seen between boys and girls when it comes to subjects like maths and science are based more on expectations than abilities. As girls have continued to achieve in all aspects of education, and begun to see themselves differently, these traditional differences are fading. We'll talk more about school in Chapter 10, but for now take comfort from the fact there is now plenty of good evidence that girls can do maths just as well as boys can.

Yeah, yeah, but . . .

The problem with me saying all this is that it kind of goes against the grain, don't you think? It seems that I'm arguing for the case that boys and girls are the same, when any idiot can see that they aren't. You only need to walk into any playground and spend a few minutes watching kids play to see that boys and girls do seem to be quite different in how they go about most things. As a general rule, the boys are running around yelling, and the girls are standing around talking. A gross generalization, I know, but it has a ring of truth about it.

I'm not saying that girls and non-girls are the same; I'm saying that finding neuroscience-based explanations for those differences is not as clear-cut as some people would have you believe. It's likely that there are going to be some neurological differences between girls and boys, but by far the most consistent pattern that seems to emerge when you dig beneath all the pseudoscience into the *actual* science is that the differences are, on average, quite small with a lot of individual variation.

Tips on

Mars, Venus, and sexual pseudoscience

☆ Always be wary when people start using neuroscience and 'brain scans' to back up their argument: it makes things sound more convincing than they are.

☆ There's a lot of hype about 'male brains' and 'female brains', but a more objective look at the science seems to show that there are small average differences, with lots of overlap.

8

Bears, dirty Scandinavian shrinks, and a revealing hypothesis

I was once almost eaten by a bear in Wisconsin. It was way back in 1994 and I'd just been to Minneapolis with some colleagues to attend a conference on treating sex offenders. The conference itself had been pretty dull, save for an extremely interesting talk by some Scandinavians. Their workshop was on 'masturbatory reconditioning', which is pretty much what the name suggests — basically, it's a way to modify a sexual offender's deviant fantasies. Up until that point, the conference had all been guys in suits talking to endless PowerPoint slides of graphs and statistics. Informative, sure, but dull to the point you almost wanted to see how far you could push a pencil up your nose before your left arm went numb and started to spasm.

Then along came the gloriously liberal, dirty Scandinavian shrinks. Instead of just talking about what they did, those crazy Europeans gave a roomful of largely American and somewhat reserved 'professionals' a slide-by-slide tour of the actual 'healthy' sexual fantasy pictures they used with their clients. It turned out that the Scandinavian definition of 'healthy' was a lot more colourful than most of the rest of the world's. Their stuff was like an LSD-fuelled rainbow sandwich of alternative lifestyles.

So our small band of quietly amused New Zealanders sat in a room that was deathly quiet — the kind of quiet that can only come from abject mortification — and tried not to giggle as the cloying silence was broken only by pained and uncomfortable shuffling of beige-trousered legs. All the while, images of transsexuals, bondage scenes, gay sex, lesbian sex, gay bondage transsexual sex, and stuff which seemed to make no sense at all were blown up into glorious 6 foot by 6 foot high-definition images.

It was one of the funniest presentations I've ever been to, even if it was funny for all the wrong reasons.

Shortly after that, we left the conference and spent the rest of the day wandering through the woods of rural Wisconsin, looking for black bears. In hindsight, I don't know why we did this, apart from the vague idea that it would be pretty cool to see one. We didn't, but I am convinced they were watching us, and I'm convinced we were almost eaten. I have no actual evidence of that. It's just a feeling.

What is even more interesting is that, if I'd hung about for another 11 years, I could have stopped in at the University of Wisconsin and met with Professor Janet Shibley Hyde, who developed a very interesting, and very relevant hypothesis which is as reassuring as it is confusing.

We didn't hang about for 11 years. In fact we flew out the next day and went off to blues clubs in Chicago, and then on to New York, where, like all tourists, we wandered about both impressed and completely paranoid about being shot dead by muggers. I love America. I always have, even through the George W Bush years when everyone hated America. Even when it wasn't cool to love America, I still did. President Obama made it cool again in 2009, but some of us were there even before Obama beat Sarah Palin and that other guy. How can you not love a place that makes such fantastic doughnuts?

All that aside, I wish I had spoken with Professor Hyde, because the paper she published in 2005 is, in my opinion, a pretty remarkable testament to the fact that men and women are a long way from being a long way apart. In fact, she clearly demonstrated that we're far more alike than we are different.

How she did that was to analyse the reviews of all the research looking at male and female attributes that had been done so far. In scientific journals there are, broadly speaking, two types of papers that people write: the first are papers which describe an individual piece of research (say, an experiment looking at the performance of males versus females in abstract reasoning); the second are papers which provide a review of a large number of papers on a particular area (again, say, abstract reasoning) to see what the 'big picture' is when you look at all the papers which have examined that particular topic. What Professor Hyde did was essentially to review the reviews of studies of gender-based attributes and abilities, cunningly termed a 'meta-review', to see what the '*big* big picture' was when you looked at the whole kit and caboodle.

Professor Hyde then statistically analysed the results of research reviews, looking at 128 different abilities/attributes. And this is where it gets interesting, and where it is hugely relevant to the everyday life of dads raising daughters, because if you listened to all the Mars and Venus pop psychology that goes on, the results would clearly show that boys and girls are as different as chocolate buttons and chilli beans.

Which is why what she found was so gosh-diddly-darned surprising: a total of 82% of the psychological variables/attributes showed *no difference* between males and females. Out of this overwhelming majority of variables which showed no difference, the following 23 examples are a small sample of some of the areas where the gentlemen and the ladies came out even:

◊ mathematics

◊ reading comprehension

◊ vocabulary

◊ science

◊ attributions of success and failure in tasks
◊ talkativeness (in children)
◊ facial expression processing
◊ negotiation outcomes
◊ helping behaviour
◊ leadership style
◊ neuroticism
◊ openness
◊ life satisfaction
◊ self-esteem
◊ happiness
◊ depression symptoms
◊ coping
◊ moral reasoning
◊ computer use
◊ job preference for challenge
◊ job preference for security
◊ job preference for earnings
◊ job preference for power.

There were 11% of the psychological variables where there was a *moderate difference* between males and females, and these were as follows (greater effect size for males or females indicated in parentheses):

◊ spelling (females)
◊ language (females)
◊ mental rotation (males)
◊ spatial perception (males)
◊ smiling (females)

◊ smiling: aware of being observed (females)

◊ aggression: all types (males)

◊ physical aggression (males)

◊ verbal aggression (males)

◊ extroversion: assertiveness (males)

◊ body esteem (males)

◊ sprinting (males)

◊ activity level (males)

◊ computer self-efficacy (males).

A total of 5.5 % of the psychological variables examined in the various reviews showed a *large difference* between males and females:

◊ mechanical reasoning (males)

◊ spatial visualization (males)

◊ physical aggression (males), in some studies

◊ helping whilst being observed (males)

◊ masturbation (females . . . no, just kidding, it really was the males)

◊ attitudes to casual sex (males)

◊ agreeableness: tender-mindedness (females)

◊ grip strength (males).

And what do you think the *very large differences* between males and females were? When all the studies of all the stuff that boys and girls do was stacked up, measured, catalogued, and gently placed in a little bottle of formalin for the entertainment and edification of small children on field trips to Dr Phibe's Gruesome Museum of Freaky Scientific Wonders, the two biggest differences between the sexes were these:

◊ the speed an object is thrown (males)

◊ how far the object is thrown (males).

So what that means is that, if you have a large group of people and you want to sort them out into girls and boys without actually looking at them, the best way would be to get them all to throw a ball. Put the half who can throw it the furthest and the fastest in one group, and the other lot are likely to be mostly girls.

Moral of the story

If there were a moral to this story, it would be this: we're far more like our daughters than we are different. If it were really true that we were all from different planets, you'd expect to see the numbers the other way around, with 82% of the attributes showing a large difference and only 2% being no different. This is a really important point to understand in my view, because it means that — high heels and fairy obsessions notwithstanding — our daughters aren't quite as alien as they might at first appear. Sure there are differences, but fundamentally we are far more alike than different. She sees the same world that you do, she hears the same things, she is able to do many of the same things that you do.

Yeah, yeah — so how come they feel so bloody different?

Good question, and it comes back to where we began: high heels and zombies. There are differences between the ladies and the gentlemen that seem to go beyond just footwear. It's all very well to say that we share pretty similar brains, and that we have fairly similar attributes and abilities, but that doesn't really satisfy.

It feels a bit . . . you know . . . limp.

So what's all that about, then?

Well, it seems that there are some interesting differences

that exist between men and women, but the closer you get to elephants, the more they disappear.

Tips on
Bears, dirty Scandinavian shrinks, and . . .

☆ When you look at what the research tells us about the differences between males' and females' abilities and attributes, it seems that we're far more similar than different.

☆ Differences have emerged, but there are far more similarities between the sexes.

☆ Although your daughter might seem like she's from a different planet, she isn't. She's far more like you than she is different.

9

Personality development, gender differences, and why elephants are the great levellers

Some girls are sweet, and some are not. In fact, some girls are so much the opposite of sweet that they can set a room ablaze with one well-placed sneer.

Katey was like that. She was 13 and had the ability to turn a nice moment into a complete disaster without missing a beat. She was like a one-girl destructive force of Nature. If this were a *Star Wars* movie, she would have been called Darth Katey. If it were an *X-Men* movie, she would have been called Screamerine. If it could burn, she'd torch it; and if it couldn't, she'd keep trying until she found a way.

She was *good*.

Her parents were distraught. They couldn't work out what they'd done wrong, because her little sister was such an easy kid. So they'd come to see me, without the kids, to try to figure it out.

'I just don't know what she's thinking,' her father said.

I shrugged, 'Tom, you wouldn't be the first dad I've heard use that line.'

Mary, Katey's hapless mother, sat beside her husband looking completely done-in. She just shook her head sadly, much as one would if one were talking about a child who had been lost during a space walk at the international space station, which, thanks to Wolfram Alpha (a pretty cool search engine), I now know was 18,000 kilometres over the Philippines at that precise moment.

'I don't understand how Sally can be so nice, and Katey can be such a . . . such a . . .' he trailed off, unsure how to finish the sentence.

'Demonic she-bitch from hell?' I suggested helpfully.

He laughed, but in an 'it's-funny-because-it's-true' kind of way. 'Yeah. I mean from day one Sally's been such an easy kid. She does what she's told, she never really gets that upset about anything, she does her jobs without complaining . . . But Katey — good God.'

'Would I be far off the mark in thinking that Katey's been stubborn from the very beginning?'

They both nodded.

'I'd even bet she was stubborn in the womb.'

Mary smiled, for the first time. 'She was, actually. If I lay the wrong way, she'd kick until I moved.'

'And she was always quite particular about how she wanted things done?'

Nodding.

'And when she wanted things done?'

Nodding.

'And it was bearable, only just, but bearable, right up until she hit adolescence?'

Emphatic nodding.

'That's what I would have thought. Well, the good news is that she will grow out of this, or at least she'll start to mellow a little.'

They both seemed to visibly relax a little. 'Thank God,' breathed Tom. 'When?'

I thought for a moment or two. 'About 50-ish.'

And it was like I'd dropped a cup of cold sick right in the middle of the room.

Of course, that wasn't the whole story. She would start to mellow significantly when she hit her 50s (although her parents would probably be dead by then, so it was scant comfort to them), but they could expect things to improve quite a bit before then. Still, if you start off at 50 and then tell people that things will actually start to change a little sooner, the sense of relief is a lot greater.

Personality and the 'Big Five'

It would have been much cooler if psychologists studying personality had identified a 'Big Three' — mostly because three is a far cooler number than five — but they didn't. For some reason researchers seem far more interested in trying to accurately describe what they find rather than in coolness. This is, I suppose, a good thing because the science is more robust, but it's a real bummer for those of us trying to spin the coolness of science.

The Big Five might be more accurate, but the Big Three is just cooler.

Now, all that aside, I'm sure you'd probably like to know what the Big Five are. Fair enough. Psychologists have been interested in personality for a very long time. The reason for that is pretty obvious, in that 'personality' is an essential part of who we are; in some ways it's the biggest part, since this shapes how we see and experience the world, and in turn how others experience us.

If someone tells you that the new guy is kind of grumpy and stubborn, then you instantly know a lot about him. Mostly you know that you're not going to want to spend a lot of time around him. Similarly, if they say that the new boss is a nice guy but a bit of a stickler for details, then you know that you're in for a bit of a mixed ride. All this is the stuff of personality; it's the traits and foibles that make us who we are.

Whilst psychologists are notorious for disagreeing about things, one of the areas where there seems to be some agreement is in the area of personality research. It's now fairly well accepted that there are five 'superfactors' which paint a broad picture of adult personality structure. These are as follows:

1. X-ray vision

2. superhuman strength

3. invulnerability

4. super-stretchy limbs

5. telekinesis.

Actually, that's not really true. Again, it would be cool if it were, but sadly superfactors aren't things like X-ray vision and telekinesis. In reality, superfactors are the higher-order broad traits which define our personalities. Within each of these broad traits researchers have described lower-order traits which help to fine-tune the picture, but I don't want to muddy the water too much, so for now let me briefly outline these 'superfactors', this time for real.

1 *Extroversion/positive emotionality*
This describes the tendency for a person to be actively and positively involved in their world. Extroverted people are bold, outgoing, and energetic (ie, farters). At the other end of this superfactor, people are introverted, quiet, meek, inhibited, and lethargic (ie, non-farters).

2 *Neuroticism/negative emotionality*
This superfactor relates to a person's susceptibility to experience negative feelings, to get distressed, and to feel anxious, vulnerable, or guilt-prone. This one's all about how wound up about stuff you get.

3 *Conscientiousness/constraint*
This superfactor describes the tendency for people to vary in their ability to control their thoughts and their behaviours. People high on this superfactor are

responsible, attentive, persistent, and generally have their shit completely together. If you're low on this trait, you tend to be irresponsible, careless, and distractible.

4 *Agreeableness*
This superfactor involves a whole cluster of traits that determine if you're nice to be around, or a bit of a pain. If you're high on this one, then you tend to be co-operative, considerate, and empathetic. Low on this and you're more aggressive, rude, spiteful, and manipulative.

5 *Openness to experience/intellect*
This superfactor is the most debated of all the superfactors — mostly because researchers are still arguing over the small print for this one — but basically it describes your tendency to be imaginative and creative, and how quick to learn and insightful you are.

Using these five superfactors as an organizing framework, researchers have learned a whole bunch of interesting things about what makes us who we are, and, of particular relevance to you and me, some interesting things about personality differences between the sexes. Essentially, the personality research bears out the old stereotypes that dads are more likely to let you jump out of a tree, and mums are more likely to tell you to be careful. It turns out that, at a general level, men tend to be more assertive and take more risks, while women tend to be more anxious than men and more tender-minded. What's really interesting is that these sex differences in personality are able to be detected in childhood and remain fairly constant across the lifespan.

So there does seem to be some scientific support for the notion that men make better pirates. Cool, huh?

Remember, though, all those things that we talked about in earlier chapters about how most of these scientific 'facts' are more accurately described as small average differences with a lot of variation. So, while it's a great line to drop at parties that there is scientific support for the position that men make better pirates, at the individual level this stuff isn't cut-and-dried. Sure there might be some anxious girls, but there are also reckless, thrill-seeking girls as well.

Elephants are the great levellers

Now here's where it gets really interesting, because researchers have also found that as you go from prosperous countries to less-developed countries these sex differences in personality become less extreme. This doesn't mean that these countries are any more egalitarian than us — in fact some of them are very restrictive in their views of women and women's roles in society — but what does seem to happen is that men and women become more alike in how their personalities are expressed.

The big question is why?

My rather sophisticated and cunning theory is that it's the elephants. If you think about it, how many elephants are there in the developed world? Not many, right? You don't often see elephants roaming Fifth Avenue in New York, or circling Picca-dilly Circus in London, or hanging out in the shopping malls of Wollongong in Australia, or even the Oamaru Botanic Gardens in New Zealand. You will not often meet an elephant queuing up outside the Colosseum in Rome (although that might be more to do with bad associations that elephants have with the various Caesars). You will also hardly ever see an elephant wandering the cobbled streets of Prague, or the bustling metropolis of Taipei.

But how many elephants are there in developing nations?

Heaps.

Buckets of them. They're out there roaming the savannahs, and the rainforests, and the less-rainy forests.

In my view, elephants have a sobering effect on people. Just the sight of an elephant ambling along is enough to stop a crowd. They're big, and grey, and they don't take any shit. I think the elephants just don't like the notion of gender differences in personality, and so they step in and break it up.

Of course, the academics have some really dull theory that the reason why sex differences become more extreme in wealthier countries is that men and women have more equal access to education and the ability to prosper economically, and so have the time, money, and resources to do their own thing a little more. Gender differences in personality seem to be a luxury item.

Dull, huh?

Which is why I'm sticking with my elephant theory.

A grand scientific adventure

In 1972 a group of researchers at the University of Otago in Dunedin, New Zealand, had an interesting idea. They wondered what they might learn if they asked all the parents of the babies born in the city that year to come in so that they could study these new wee people. They sent out some letters, and to their great surprise the families of all the babies born in the city that year — 1,037 new little people to be precise — agreed to participate in the study.

A couple of years later, when the babies were aged five, they sent out a letter again, just to see what they could learn now that the kids were a little further down the track. Incredibly, something like 96% of the original group returned. The things the researchers learned about the changes the children went through over those few years were pretty darned interesting.

What's even more amazing was that the chief researcher, an incredibly resourceful, tenacious, and passionate man called Professor Phil Silva, wondered what it would be like if they just kept going . . .

Forever.

It's a testament to Phil Silva's passion and dedication to the study, and to that of the many researchers who have come along after him, that some 37 years later they are still going. Now the study is headed up by the equally passionate Professor Richie Poulton, who has the unique responsibility of overseeing one of the grandest scientific adventures in the history of the world.

What makes it such a big deal is that every three years they bring all the study members who are still alive and able to travel back to Dunedin for several days of testing and questioning on everything from their relationships to their blood pressure and the state of their gums. It is a truly multidisciplinary study involving psychologists, dentists, doctors, and researchers of every shape and form from all over the globe. If people can't travel — like original study members who might be in jail, for instance — then the researchers go to them.

Incredibly, at the last testing phase, when the study members were aged 35, a total of 96% of these 1970s babies took part in that round of evaluations. To put that in perspective, you need to understand that in most longitudinal studies the number of people still in the study after this length of time is somewhere around 30% to 40%, which means that you've lost the majority of your group for all kinds of reasons that you'll never know. In the Dunedin study, almost everyone who's still alive is still in.

And that's huge.

The Dunedin Multidisciplinary Health and Development Study (DMDHDS), as it is now known, is peeling back the layers of what makes us who we are. I've included in the endnotes section at the back of this book a link to their website, so you can go and have a look at just a small sample of some of the amazing research they've been producing for the past 37 years. It is a truly unique insight into how the events of our lives, both great and small, affect us all. For that alone we owe both the researchers and the study participants an enormous debt of gratitude, because they are helping us to understand what makes us who we are. This is the study of lives lived on a scale that is truly awe-inspiring.

Teach your girl how to drive her personality

There are some particularly relevant findings from the DMDHDS that I think can be of great assistance to those of us raising kids. Researchers at the DMDHDS found that there were five separate styles of behavioural presentations evident in the children at age three, and that these behavioural styles predicted how the children would be doing in many aspects of their life 23 years later. What this means is that we can use this rigorously tested science as a handy little compass to guide us in the particular skills we can teach our children.

I've always talked about personality as being like a car. At birth, we all get given a particular car, each one of which will have its strengths and its weaknesses, and so our job is to teach our children how to drive to their strengths, and how to manage their weaknesses. None of us is perfect, we have our strengths and we have the things which tend to trip us up a little.

Having said that, it's also important to understand that, as always, none of this stuff is absolute. She doesn't have to fit in only one box, because, like most kids, she'll probably have elements of various boxes. This stuff is just a guide, just a suggestion of a way forward. Never make the mistake of thinking that any map can tell you where to put your feet. It can't. If you want to know where the best place to put your feet is, then you need to make sure you look where you're actually going.

What follows, then, is a description of these five separate styles that the researchers at the DMDHDS found, and my suggestions about some of things you may want to teach your girl to help her drive her personality as best she can.

Under-controlled

These girls tend to be irritable, impulsive, generally grumpy, and lack persistence when it comes to completing tasks. They often don't like having a go at something new, and if they do have a go, they will usually make a fairly grumpy, half-hearted attempt and then give up in a bit of a huff. As you can probably imagine, this is not the most positive of approaches to life, and if left unchecked over the longer term is going to make for a fairly high level of grumpiness and a fairly low level of contentment. Bearing that in mind, here are my suggestions for how you help girls who behave in these kinds of ways.

◊ First off, you need to help her learn how to chill the heck out and not get so wound up about stuff. She needs to learn that the world is far from perfect and shit is going to happen, so there's nothing to be gained from getting all het up about it. Life is really annoying sometimes: if she can learn to accept that and not fight it, then it will all become a little easier to manage.

◊ Making friends is a big issue for these girls, so she is going to need lots of coaching in how to make friends. She will especially need help to understand how her behaviour has an impact on other people, because she needs to understand that if she's grumpy and sulky then it's going to be hard for her to make and keep friends.

◊ If she has a tendency towards always seeing things in very negative terms, she will need help to be more flexible in how she interprets other people's reactions to her. She will need help to find ways to understand her peers' responses to her. The simplest way to do this is by asking her something like: 'Well it could be that Suzy doesn't like you, but what other reasons do you think there could be for her not choosing you for her team?'

◊ Learning to manage impulsiveness is important for these kids. You can do this by rewarding self-control in situations that you set up (like telling her that if she saves her pocket money for two weeks then you will lend her the extra money she needs to buy the better toy).

◊ Bottom line here is that these girls need to relax, to not take everything personally, to develop a more flexible way of thinking about life, and to learn that things don't always go their way and that's OK. In fact it's a good thing, because then they get to learn more and to stretch themselves into a bigger world.

Inhibited

These girls tend to be shy, fearful, and socially ill at ease. They prefer to follow rather than lead, and retire quietly to the background, watching rather than joining in. It's worth remembering that almost all children are inhibited at various points in their lives, and that this is both normal and actually quite adaptive. Sometimes you're better to keep quiet and watch until you've worked out what's going on. Having said that, for some children stepping out into the bold, bright light of the world is a little more difficult than it is for others. If you have one of those girls, here are a few suggestions to help them on their way.

◊ Give her lots of practice at being loud and bright in the safety and comfort of her own home. Make her world-famous in her own room, and then build little bridges out from there into the rest of her life.

◊ If she has an interest in things like music, encourage it to the max. Let her sing through the piano, or the violin, or the drums. The instrument gives her a role she can play, and that can give her a presence in the world she may have struggled to find by herself.

◊ Encourage her to do reckless, dangerous things. She needs to be encouraged, cajoled, and bribed into stepping out on the highwire as much as she can stand.

◊ Help her to see that she will need to speak up for what she wants. If she doesn't, all she'll ever get is other people's leftovers. She needs your encouragement and support to use the strong voice inside her.

◊ Watch movies like *Gandhi* with her, so she can see that it isn't always the noisiest people who make the biggest differences in the world. Sometimes the people with the softest voices are the ones we all hear.

◊ Bottom line here is that she's going to need help to find her feet, to plant them firmly on the ground, and to stand that ground when the stakes are important to her. She needs to find her voice and how to use it. Your role in that is fundamentally important.

Confident

These girls are their own parade. They are zealous, outgoing, bold, and completely believe their own hype. These are the girls who say the kinds of things that other kids wouldn't dream of saying. 'Gumption' is something they have in buckets. All this is mostly good, of course, but too much of anything is hardly ever a good thing, and this is just as true of gumption as it is for everything else. So here are my suggestions for helping these girls to steer a slightly smoother path.

◊ Humility will not come naturally to these girls, so you'll need to work pretty hard to teach them its value. It's terrific that they think they're so great, but other people will find that annoying after a while. What is cute in little girls very quickly becomes utterly boring in young women.

◊ Along with humility, it may help to teach them to exercise a little impulse control. Confidence is fantastic, but over-confidence usually leads to disaster and heartbreak. Stopping and thinking it all through is something these girls need to learn.

◊ It also may help them to learn that, while they can get a

lot of attention and adulation for being brash and 'out there', there is also something to be said for being a little conventional from time to time. People who are always 'out there' can be very wearying for the rest of us, so give them the gift of pacing and you will be doing them a great favour.

Reserved

It's hardly surprising to know that girls who fall into this group are . . . well . . . reserved. They aren't completely paralysed with doubt, but tend to hang back. Their approach to some new situation is to get a little anxious and pull back. Again, we all tend to be a little like this in different contexts, and so there's nothing innately wrong with this approach *per se*. The problems obviously begin if this is your girl's approach to most new situations.

◊ She needs to learn that there's nothing wrong with making mistakes; in fact, making mistakes is one of the most important things you have to do in life. If you don't make mistakes, you're not learning anything.

◊ Actively work to change her associations about failing or not knowing what to do. You can do this by showering her with praise when she does make a mistake. Use this as a time to really get to grips with the cool stuff she's learned about herself and the problem.

◊ Have a turn at the dinner table where everyone describes 'the best mistake I made today'.

◊ Help her to understand that there are few mistakes which will actually result in the end of the world. Most times, the sky does not fall.

◊ Bottom line is that she needs to learn not to take life so seriously — even the most serious bits should rarely be taken seriously.

Well-adjusted

These girls are about as low-maintenance as they come. They have a go at most things in an age-appropriate way, and don't get wound up about unimportant things. They seem to understand that shit happens from time to time, and so just deal with it and move on. Low in drama and high on good nature, these girls are what we all want. They're not perfect, but they tend to be fairly capable and even-handed in their approach to life. These are my suggestions if you have one of these.

◊ Thanks the gods that you have been blessed with such an easy kid. Light scented candles and sacrifice goats to the gods — whatever it takes to curry their continuing good favour.

◊ Take all the credit. Make sure people know that her even-tempered nature is all down to your competence as a parent.

◊ Give everyone else advice on how they can raise a child as perfect as yours. Most likely your advice will be useless, because your daughter's good nature is probably as much about her genes as it is about your parenting.

◊ Have fun. Just have lots and lots of fun.

Personality development throughout the lifespan

The good news is that our personalities continue to develop over the course of our entire lives. While the basic structure of who we are remains relatively intact, it seems that we do mellow with age. Life bends and shapes us, and wisdom seeps into our bones without us really having to consciously think about it. In fact it seems that personality development is much more stable during childhood and adolescence than most of us would have thought. What should be at least a little comforting is that there is good evidence that teenagers become more agreeable and emotionally stable as they get older — and the news gets even better for you, because it also seems that girls mature in this way earlier than boys.

It isn't until early adulthood that the most significant changes occur. It seems that those first few years when you leave home are when you finally have the freedom to be who you really are. So her first few years away from home are when she finally has the freedom to stretch her wings and be who she really is in a purposeful and conscious way.

Personality traits continue to develop in boys and girls, and reach a peak somewhere after we hit age 50. It seems we really do mellow with age, which is something nice to look forward to. In any case, the big message is that change is inevitable. There is some great comfort to be taken from this if you're worried about your daughter's attitude and approach to life. It will change. How much, in what form, and how long this takes will vary from person to person, but change *will* occur. It is inevitable.

So sometimes all you can do is just dig in, and wait.

Tips on

Personality development, gender difference, and elephants

☆ There do seem to be some differences in male and female personality traits.

☆ Males tend to be more assertive and take more risks.

☆ Females tend to be more anxious than men and more tender-minded.

☆ Those are just general trends, though, and there will always be exceptions to the rule.

☆ What's more, those sex differences in personality become less marked as you go from more-developed nations to less-developed nations.

☆ This may be related to elephants.

☆ Your job is to teach your daughter to drive the personality that she's got.

10

Girls are more school-friendly

If you're the father of a daughter, then there's good news a-plenty for you here. The big picture for girls is that they're actually doing really well in school, and there are all kinds of indices which show this. In fact, girls have been doing so well in comparison with boys that a lot of people have started to worry that now boys are having some sort of crisis. My analysis of all that — which I've written about in *Mothers Raising Sons* — is that it isn't so much that boys are doing badly, it's more that girls are improving a lot faster. Which is good news for the parents of girls.

Single-sex or co-ed?

The first thing you need to know about this particular debate is that it's Ground Zero for all the sexual pseudoscience nonsense. This is where all that boy/girl brain stuff starts to yap like a yappy little dog behind a big fence with a really big dog on the other side. This is where you'll hear all the jiminy-himiny about how girls' hearing is much more sensitive than boys' hearing, and their eyes are hardwired completely differently, and their brains develop much more quickly, and all that bumf. Let's face it, the sexual pseudoscience was expressly developed to further the cause of single-sex schools, and particularly to further the cause of single-sex education for boys, particularly given all the 'boy crisis' rhetoric that we talked about earlier.

Of course, by now hopefully you've read enough in here to make you a little sceptical about all that. With any luck, you're a *lot* sceptical about it all.

So what does the research say about single-sex education? Is it better for girls or not? It will probably come as no great surprise to you that if you go surfing the web you will find websites which quote all manner of studies which appear to have concluded beyond a shadow of a doubt that single-sex education is by far and away best for girls and boys. However, as we've already seen with the sexual pseudoscience stuff, it does always pay to dig a little deeper to see what's underneath the initial hype.

When I set about swimming around in the sea of research papers published in this area, it was very personal. I was writing the education chapter of *Mothers Raising Sons*, and, having two boys, I had a big personal stake in seeing what the science could tell me about whether single-sex education or co-education was best for kids. I wanted to know what was best for my boys, just as you want to know what is best for your girl(s).

As it turned out, the answer — in my opinion, having now looked at quite a lot of the actual research for myself — is pretty much the same for the both of us. Now, I'm aware that there are going to be people who would disagree with my analysis of what the research means for everyday parenting, so I'm going to lay it all out in the open for you here so you can see how I got to that point.

◊ There are a number of studies, and these are probably the larger number, which have shown that girls achieve higher grades in single-sex schools.

◊ There are also studies which have shown only very small differences in achievement, and studies which have shown no real advantages or differences in actual achievements.

◊ The problem is that there are always a range of other factors at play, which means that these results should be viewed with caution — including the fact that many of the single-sex schools featuring in research papers are private, whereas many of the co-ed schools are public.

◊ When you take all those differences into account, a lot of the observed advantages seem to disappear.

◊ One theme that does seem to consistently emerge from research findings over time is that girls are more likely to engage in non-traditional subjects like maths and science in a single-sex environment.

The big message here about single-sex versus co-ed schools for girls is that the picture is slightly murky. While there have been studies which have shown girls have achieved better in single-sex schools, there are a lot of confounding variables — like social class, parental circumstances, and private versus public comparisons — that make it hard to make any definitive statements about which is best.

So, what are we to make of all this?

In my view — and certainly this has been my experience when working with many schools and many educators from all over the world — the *quality* of the school is far more important than whether or not it's co-ed or single sex. One good principal can make a huge difference to the quality of education your child receives, far more than either the presence or the absence of boys. For sure, there does seem to be some evidence of some advantages for girls in a single-sex education environment, but in my view these are not significant enough to make the statement that this means *all* girls will do better in *all* single-sex schools. I'd choose a good co-ed school with a good management team over an average single-sex school any day of the week.

The preschool years

Some parents get wound up about these early years and try to cram in every intellectually stimulating activity they can, but I'd suggest that it's probably not worth the hassle. Certainly the early years are important years in terms of brain development — we've all heard that over and over. Mostly because it's true. The early years *are* important, but it isn't like she needs a rigorous programme of intellectual stimulation to get through it. All she needs is warm, consistent care.

That's it.

In fact, assuming the warm, consistent care is part of the everyday backdrop of her life — and if you're the kind of dad who reads parenting books, then I think that's a pretty safe assumption — what she *really* needs most is to have fun. This is a fantastic time in kids' lives, and you should try to enjoy it as much as you possibly can. It's also a time when they enjoy their life as much as they possibly can.

Don't choose a preschool based on which one spends the most time teaching her things like reading, and writing, and maths. She doesn't need to get a jump-start on school. The only thing she needs to be jumping is rope. Choose a preschool on the basis that the teachers are nice, the facilities are good, and the emphasis is on having fun.

The first day of school

Usually this one is a lot harder on mums than it is on dads, but even for us it's a bit of a thing. It's a happy day, but it's always tinged with the slightly sad realization that this is when she begins to head off into her own life. Still, on the bright side, she will be gone from 9am until 3pm, so that does leave a bit more peace and quiet during the day.

In recent years the first day of school has become a major

production, involving months of planning and carefully timetabled execution. In my humble old opinion, it's all got a little over-the-top. Sometimes you'd think the kids were off for a six-month deployment in Iraq, given all the hoop-lah that precedes the first day. I think kids are pretty robust as a general rule, and much of the little person's first-day jitters can often be traced back to parental anxiety.

So here are my suggestions for starting school.

◊ Start talking about how cool school is, early on — pretty much as soon as they're old enough to grasp the concept. Make it something cool to look forward to once they're older.

◊ At the weekends it can help to go down to your local school to play a bit, so they will get familiar with where everything is.

◊ Some school visits before they start can also help. One or two is fine. There's no need to be there every week for months.

◊ Just prior to the first day, go out and let them choose a schoolbag and a school lunchbox. Rituals are important and help to build the anticipation.

◊ When the day arrives, keep it all upbeat but low-key. It should be an exciting day, not an anxious day.

◊ If you are feeling anxious: bluff.

◊ Leave for school with plenty of time so you don't have to rush.

◊ When you get there, help her to get settled in, stay just long enough to meet the teacher and make sure everything is good, then leave. Don't hang around for hours, because all that says is that it's too much for her to cope with by herself.

◊ If she starts to cry, then diplomatically pass her over to the teacher and leave. Most teachers of new entrants (or Year One kids) are very good at settling upset little people. The longer you stay, the worse it usually is.

If you have real problems, then you will invariably find that the classroom teacher is a good resource for helping sort the problem out. It's quite normal for little kids to get upset at some point when you leave, but so long as you keep calm, and keep on with it, she'll eventually get the message that school isn't a big deal, and also that she is more than able to cope with it.

The early years in school
(5–10 years)

The single most important thing to do with girls during these years, I think, is simply to help them learn to love learning. The world is changing so rapidly that continuous learning is now a part of all our lives, so if her early associations with learning are positive then you're 75% of the way there. Fortunately, as we talked about before, girls seem to be doing particularly well in school and are actually improving faster than boys. Girls, at a general level, seem to be more suited to the school environment in lots of ways and don't struggle with some of the issues boys do (eg, sitting still, not talking in class, paying attention).

Probably the biggest thing she will have to deal with in school is the social nastiness of the girl-world, which we're going to talk about next in Chapter 11. As a parent, your biggest issues at this point are probably the things you shouldn't do. To make it easier, I've listed my key 'not to do's' below.

◊ Don't be a whiny parent. Teachers hate parents who come in and whine all the time about every last little thing that happens. Don't be one. By all means go in if you are really worried — and in fact teachers do you want you to do this

— just don't go in and complain, question, and harass the teacher over every last little thing.

◊ Don't get all anxious and over-the-top about learning. Learning should be fun, not a chore; so take an interest, by all means, ask her questions and get her to explain stuff she's learned — just don't push it to the point where she's getting fed up or you'll end up teaching her that learning sucks.

◊ Don't solve every last little problem for her. She needs to learn how to be independent and deal with things by herself, and the way you teach her that is to let her practise when she's little.

◊ Don't go in and rescue her if she gets in trouble. It's important that kids learn about actions and consequences, and the way you do that is to let them experience the consequences of their actions.

◊ Don't run down the school or the teacher in front of her. Ever. It's obvious, I know, but sometimes people forget the importance of things which might seem patently obvious.

Remember, at this age it's all about building confidence and a sense of mastery. The easiest way to do that is to show her that you believe she can deal with problems by letting her deal with problems, by backing her up when she needs it, and, above all, by making the whole school thing fun.

The teen years
(11–19 years)

This is, perhaps not surprisingly, where it can get a little trickier. It's about here that the battles for control can sometimes begin, and if they do then school tends to be one of the frontlines. The big advantage that you have with a daughter is that she's liable to talk to you about what she thinks a lot more than boys this age will. You may not always agree with what she's thinking, but you are more likely to know what she's thinking, which can only be a good thing.

◊ This is where you have to really start getting your head around the fact that she is going to make more and more decisions for herself from here on in.

◊ Like all parents of teenagers, you're going to have to work that delicate balance between encouraging her to study and giving her enough room to do things her own way. This will not always be your way, but she needs to find her own place in the world, and school is a big part of her world.

◊ Try to make her space as learning-friendly as possible. Make sure she has a good desk and a light, and that the area is warm enough.

◊ The good news is that girls tend to be more studious than boys, and they also tend not to leave things until the last minute to quite the same extent that boys do.

◊ If she hasn't finished projects on time, don't go into school and try to get her extra time. The last thing she needs is her dad wading in on her behalf. Her behalf is her behalf.

In the unhappy circumstance that she takes no interest in school and wants to leave, often there isn't a lot you can do about it. If she doesn't want to, she doesn't want to — and usually the more you push, the more you increase that desire to leave. If she does 'drop out', all you can do is make sure she knows she can't just laze around: she has to get a job, and she has to start paying board.

It's also important to think about the fact that dropping out at 16 doesn't mean dropping out forever. There are almost as many ways back into the education system as there are out. She might want to drop out and stack shelves in supermarkets now, but chances are that six months to a year later she might be finding that a little dull. Plenty of girls, and boys too for that matter, follow a winding road to career happiness.

The easy bit
(age 20 onwards)

This is where it all gets easier for most of us. This is usually when everything calms down a bit, because they are now running their own life. By this stage, your role has shifted to that of an occasional consultant. If you're lucky, and if you've played your cards right during the early years, she'll still come to you for advice. So your job at this point is simply to be a sounding board. Offer an opinion, but make sure she knows that it's just an opinion and that she has to figure out her own course.

Tips on
Why girls are more school-friendly

☆ Girls are generally doing pretty well in schools.

☆ A number of studies show that girls tend to perform better in single-sex schools, but there are also studies which say the opposite.

☆ Pick the best school you can, based on a number of factors (like having a good management team, positive school culture, etc). If that's a single-sex school, great. If it's co-ed, that's fine too.

11

'Mean girls' — the new cult of bitchiness

It's hard to get away from the 'mean girl' phenomenon these days. Mean girls are now solidly part of popular culture. They've even had their own film. The technical term for meanness in this context is 'relational violence/aggression', but really this is just the polite way that scientists and academics say 'bitchiness'. If you have girls, then it's likely you will hear more and more about 'relational violence', so it's worth us pausing just for a moment to look at where it all came from.

When 'mean girls' were invented

'Relational aggression' wasn't discovered until the 1990s, when a Swedish researcher first started studying whether girls are as aggressive as boys. This early work was picked up on by more researchers, and, before you knew it, a whole new thing had come into existence. It's important to understand this if you have girls, because psychology has a great way of inventing something which then becomes fashionable and a bit cool, and a whole bunch of people then do research, write books, and go on the lecture circuit talking about it.

Now, I'm not saying for a moment that girls weren't mean up until the 1990s, because they were. In my view, girls have always been mean. Not all girls of course, just some, and even then not all the time, but there was meanness about in the land long before the scientists started to document it. Unfortunately, psychology has a disturbing tendency to take something that is quite reasonable and sensible and then stretch it beyond all recognition or reason. All of which is why we need to exercise a little restraint when talking about mean girls. It probably isn't some new plague; it's probably stuff that's been there all the time. The big questions for us aren't in the sludgy depths of the philosophical/theoretical/political hooble-de-goobledy, but at the sharp end of parenting.

For that reason, I'm not going to get too lost in all the debate and complications surrounding this issue; I'll stick to the really pragmatic issues. It could well be that the term 'mean girl' is simply a way to regulate and pathologize normal femininity, as some have suggested — but I'm not going to get into all that, because it's all a bit too political for me. Instead, I'm going to step over it and focus on the aspects of meanness which have an impact on us as parents: namely what is it, and how do we deal with it?

What is 'relational violence'?

Like I said before, 'relational violence' is bitchiness. Plain and simple: it's girls being mean. It can take many forms:

◊ name-calling

◊ creating cliques and alliances to ostracize and reject other girls

◊ sharing information that was passed on in confidence

◊ texting nasty messages

◊ posting nasty messages on social-networking websites

◊ spreading nasty rumours

◊ intimidating and harassing

◊ pretending to be a friend and then making fun of her behind her back

◊ indulging in general, bitchy nastiness.

Relational violence comes in many different and varied forms, but the underlying thread is that the intent is to be mean. What's more, status seems to play quite a big role in both the perpetration and the impact of bitchiness. High-status girls tend to be bitchier, and the impact of their bitchiness is more intense than if a low-status girl says or does the same stuff. It's all about being popular, and so if a girl who's more popular than you is mean it has a nastier bite than a girl who's less popular than you.

Now, it has to be said that an element of meanness is present in most kids' play from time to time. Like anything else, meanness is simply a part of life, and it's hard to see how we could ever banish meanness from kids' worlds. Childhood is when children first learn about how to be mean, and about the upsides and downsides of being mean. In fact, just the presence of 'relational violence' in the everyday normal social interactions of children would tend to suggest that there has to be some kind of benefit from being 'mean'. If there weren't some payoff, surely it would fade away?

So if there is a payoff, what could it be?

Well, it seems that a little bit of meanness may help you get ahead in life. If you're socially dominant, but you're still able to control yourself and not become a complete and utter *über-bitch*, then you may be more likely to get first pick at the plate. Of course, that does have to be balanced up against the fact that research has also shown that bitchiness in childhood is related to a whole host of negative outcomes later in life, including anxiety, depression, alcohol and drug use, fear of being criticized, and self-harm. All things in moderation, maybe? Even meanness?

How can you help your daughter if she's the target of bitchiness?

For most dads, when they find out someone is picking on their daughter the first urge is to go down there and kick some butt, figuratively speaking of course. Obviously none of us would go and actually kick some little girl's butt, but we certainly would feel like kicking the little bitch's butt.

Again, can't do it, but equally can't help feeling it.

So what are your options if your girl is being targeted by the local Queen Bitch?

When kids are quite small, often a quiet word with the classroom teacher can be all that it takes. Most schools are fairly well-educated about the causes and consequences of bullying. It used to be that this stuff was ignored, but all that has changed over the past few years. It's quite common for schools to run anti-bullying programmes as part of their normal curriculum. If that doesn't bring you any joy, or the teacher doesn't seem to be handling the situation, you might want to go up the chain and talk to the principal. If you do get to this level, my standard advice about the kinds of assurances you should be thinking about are the following.

◇ How is the school going to keep your daughter safe, either from the current bullying and/or being picked on more if the other kid(s) find out that she has reported them?

◇ How will the bullies be dealt with? What remedial steps will be taken with them?

◇ How will the situation be monitored to ensure that the issues have been addressed?

◇ How will the school communicate with you about the outcomes of any investigations and/or interventions? Clearly there are confidentiality issues that the school is bound by, regarding the offending pupil, but you should at least get some general feedback about outcomes.

If you can't get good answers to these questions, keep making noises until you do. But keep in mind that it's a fine line between an involved parent and a whiny parent. Schools hate whiny parents, so make sure you've got genuine concerns before you go in and start making noises.

Also, and this is a tricky one, be prepared for the fact that you may learn that your child has actually been perpetrating some bitchiness of her own. I'm not saying that this will always be the case, but you need to be open to the possibility all the same.

Now, having said all that, the sad fact is that your daughter is going to have to learn to live with at least some degree of bitchiness. Like I said before, it may not be one of the most shining aspects of human nature, but it does seem to be relatively 'natural', if that's the right word. So you're not going to be able to shield her from all that stuff, which means you're going to have to teach her some survival skills.

◊ *Teach robustness*
Anyone who says that names will never hurt them clearly has never been called names in school. Names *do* hurt, and certainly orchestrated campaigns where everyone is calling you names can make you feel like your skin has been peeled off. Sometimes the best way to help your girl is to teach her to harden up, and tough it out. Sometimes that's all you can do, because, as the old saying goes, life can sometimes be a bitch.

◊ *Get her to do a self-defence class*
You don't want her scrapping with everyone who calls her names, but it is helpful for her to know how to apply a wrist lock, or how to dump someone twice her size. All girls (and boys) should know basic self-defence, not only for the practical aspects, but because the knowledge that you can handle yourself if things get a bit noisy brings with it a certain confidence. Bullies profile their victims, and if

your daughter feels confident in herself she's less likely to get picked on.

◊ *Make home the safe haven*

Do everything you can to make home the place she comes to to get away from all that stuff. You'll need to be careful here, because mobile phones and the internet mean that the bitchy stuff can reach into her home life if you let it. Most mobile phone companies have numbers you can ring to report harassment, just as they let you block certain numbers. Most social-networking sites also let you block people from sending and receiving messages. Get familiar with the technology and use it.

◊ *Keep talking to her*

Most of all, you need to keep talking with her so that you can stay in touch with what's going on. The girl-world is one of rapidly shifting allegiances and alliances, so it can get a little confusing at times. Just keep talking is all you can do.

Sometimes the best thing to do is run away

Hannah was only 11, but already she was learning that life sometimes sucks. She'd been having a rough time at her new school for all the usual reasons. Not only was she the new kid, but she was also from a family who weren't as well-off as those of the rest of the girls in her class. They were good people, but they didn't go to France for the school holidays — which made Hannah worthy of contempt in the eyes of the majority of her classmates. She'd been fairly well ostracized by the other girls, and had also been called names and humiliated every chance they could find.

I didn't actually see Hannah, because she had said she didn't want anyone to know about what was happening in school, including shrinks, and so her parents, Murray and Margaret, had come to see me without telling her.

'We just didn't want this to be another thing to put pressure on her,' her dad said.

Fair enough.

The thing that had really tipped the balance for them was when her mother had found a piece of paper with *I wish I was dead* written on it. That would alarm even the calmest soul – and, again, rightly so.

The school had been of little real help to date. Despite the fact that it was a private school and charged quite a lot in fees, the school had proven a bit ... well ... limp when it came to tackling the issue.

'They kept having meetings with the girls, but nothing seemed to change,' said Margaret. 'I suppose it's difficult to really get these girls to be honest and stop what they're doing, but still ..'

'What would you like them to do?' I asked.

'I'd like them to go kick those little bitches' arses,' Murray said, and I detected not even a hint of humour in his response. Again, I'd have to say fair enough.

'Fair enough,' I said, 'but given we can't do that: what else would you like to have happen?'

He shook his head. 'To be honest I'm not sure what they can do. It just seems that all these girls have it in for her.'

After discussing at some length the many meetings and conversations they'd had with the school, I tended to agree.

'OK then, so what's plan B?' I asked them both.

'We just don't know anymore,' said Margaret. 'It seems like there's nothing we can do.' At which dad crossed his arms and looked frustrated.

'What?' I asked him. He shot a look at his wife. 'What?' I repeated.

'I think she should leave the school and go to the local public one.'

'And you disagree?' I asked Margaret.

'It's just that we worked so hard to get her into _____, and it's got such a good academic programme.'

I shrugged. '_____ is a good school if you're thinking about the academic stuff, I guess. The only issue is: at what cost?'

Murray clearly had a different view. 'I think _____'s a bloody awful school,' he said. 'They might get good test results, but what the hell kind of lesson is she learning about how to treat people?'

I just sat there. I had my own view about these things, but I'd long had the policy that it's always best to wait until you're asked rather than simply inflict views on people at random.

'What do you think?' Margaret asked.

Which was pretty much my cue. 'Well, the first thing you need to understand is that this is just what I think, and there ain't no science behind it at all. It's simply an opinion. The other thing is that there's no right answer, because none of us can see the future so none of us knows what the best solution is. There's just what you do, and what comes after you do it.'

They both nodded. 'OK,' said Murray. 'So what do you think?'

'I think that sometimes you're best to get the ice cream.'

He frowned. 'Eh?'

A couple of years ago, I was with my kids in a giant maze at a place called Puzzleworld. The maze had seemed like a good idea at first, but after about 40 minutes we were all hot and tired. I could see they were losing interest in getting to the end of it, and so was I. Just then we came across one of the escape doors. It was like an exit for quitters. I could tell that my wife didn't want to be a quitter; she wanted to keep going and solve the puzzle, and she said as much. I said we should let the kids decide. So I asked them if they'd rather keep going for another 40 minutes through the hot and frustrating maze so that they could get to the other end and say they'd achieved something, or would they like to quit, leave by the quitters' exit, and go get a nice, cool, tasty, quitters' ice cream.

Murray smiled. 'What did they decide?'

'They decided that the quitters' ice cream sounded like a smarter idea than the persisters' warm glow from solving the pointless maze.'

'So you think we should change schools?' asked Margaret.

'I think sometimes you have to ask yourself if all the sweat and effort to get to the end of something is better than the quick escape and the ice cream.'

'But wouldn't that be teaching her to run away from her problems?' asked Margaret.

'Yes,' I said.

'Isn't that giving her the wrong message?

I shrugged. 'Sometimes running away is the smartest thing to do. I can't tell you if it's the best thing for Hannah right now, but I can tell you my kids really enjoyed that ice cream and they haven't decided to quit everything else when the going gets tough. They seem to take it on a case-by-case basis.'

In the end, Hannah's mum and dad talked it through some more, then they asked Hannah what she wanted to do, and she moved schools. She went to the local public school, and, last time I heard, was much happier. I think happy kids will always learn more than unhappy kids, no matter what the situation.

You might not want to teach them to run away all the time, but I think there's real value in running away some of the time.

What can you do if your daughter is the Queen Bitch?

Not a very comfortable thought, is it? Still it's something you are going to need to think about, because there's every chance that, at some point, she's going to dip her toes in the great, green, glassy pool of shiny-teethed bitchiness. It ain't pretty, but it's something you need to think through.

Mostly, what this one is about is simply staying in touch with her and what's going on in her life. *The more you know, the more you know*, as the saying goes. Actually that isn't a saying, in the sense that it isn't a popular saying because I've just made it up then. Still, it would make a good saying, because it's true. If you're taking the time to keep up with the ebb and flow of her life, you're more likely to pick up on stuff that might be of concern. Listen to how she talks about her friends and what they're up to. Use every chance you get to teach her the kinds of values you'd like her to practise out there in the world.

If you get a call from her school and you find yourself facing accusations about her behaviour, don't automatically get defensive and deny everything. Take it in and think about it before you jump in with fierce denials. Most of all, it's important to reassure her school that you take things seriously and that you're going to work with them to help resolve the issue. In situations like this, the school will be your best resource for figuring out what to do next — so work with them, not against them.

And what should you do with her? Well if she has been the bully, she needs to apologize, and there needs to be some kind of punishment. Then, when all the dust has settled, you need to make sure that you spend some time focusing on teaching her why it's wrong to be mean, and what she should be doing instead. I know that's all pretty blindingly obvious, but you'd be surprised how often parents overlook the pretty blindingly obvious, or just put it off and off to a day that never comes.

Tips on
Mean girls

☆ Girls can be pretty good at being mean, which can include everything from name-calling, to malicious gossip, to text bullying, and physical stuff as well.

☆ If your daughter is having problems, get in there and talk it through so that you can work out a plan to help her.

☆ Help her to deal with the nastiness by talking with her, getting her to do a self-defence class, helping her to 'harden up', and making home a safe sanctuary as much as you can.

☆ If your daughter is the bully, take it seriously, and get in there and make her take responsibility. Work with the school, not against them.

12

Pop culture bullshit

Sex sells. There's no way around that one — it just does. If it didn't, then we wouldn't see half-naked girls in advertisements for everything from car-exhaust systems to breakfast cereals. If fat old men sold stuff, then we'd see fat old men everywhere. Most people would spit the proverbial dummy if they saw an ad for breakfast cereal with some fat old bloke in a pair of speedos eating a plate of muesli by the swimming pool, but we don't think twice at some gorgeous blonde in a bikini munching bran flakes.

And it isn't just that, either, because popular culture has a way of making girls look a bit weak a lot of the time. Just a week ago, I was watching *The Omen* on television late one night. If you don't know what *The Omen* is then you should be a little embarrassed, because it is one of the classic horror movies of modern times. But just in case, I'll summarize it for you. The Devil's son, Damien, is adopted by an American diplomat and his wife after their own son is killed by creepy devil-worshipping nuns in an Italian hospital; then, after a series of gruesome deaths, little Damien is eventually adopted by some even more important Americans after the first lot die horribly.

If you haven't seen it, you should.

So I'm watching the birthday party scene, where little Damien's nanny goes up on the roof and jumps off with a rope around her neck, all clearly at the behest of the scary wolf that somehow manages to crash a small child's birthday party and sits about looking menacing without anyone noticing. So she jumps, and falls, and snaps to a halt all in full view of the little kiddies and their parents. There is a moment of stunned silence, and then, in true Hollywood fashion, a woman lifts her hands to her face and starts to scream and scream and scream.

Zounds!

Now if I was a girl, all that constant screaming of women in movies at the first sign of demonic mind-controlled suicide would really start to piss me off. In the movies and on television, women scream all the time, for just about any old reason. It's a complete and utter bloody nonsense, because in the real world women don't really do that — but still we're subjected to endless images of women screaming, panicking, falling over and spraining their ankles, and all manner of ridiculous girly nonsense.

There are some good role models in popular culture — like Ripley in the *Alien* series, Dana Scully from *The X Files*, Whoopi Goldberg in just about every role she's ever played, Lisa on *The Simpsons*, and a few others — but there's also a lot of crap. Most of our girls are growing up watching MTV reality shows where annoying, dizzy airheads bitch and fight and whine over things as important as who said what to whom about who has a big butt.

There are little girls who really think Paris Hilton is cool.

A large part of the message is that you have to be pretty to be important, and that you need boys to save the day. Most of all: if in doubt, just scream and scream and scream.

Sigh.

The problem for dads raising daughters is how to immunize your girls against many of the really crappy messages flying around out there about women. If you have a television, or access to the internet, or if you have neither of those things but you simply go outside from time to time, then you're going to come across these messages all the time, and so will she.

So what can you do about it?

You fight back, and you start early.

Teach her that the world is an evil place full of people who want nothing more than the total global eradication of everything that is good about the human race

It's important to understand that I am not talking about zombies here; in fact I am talking about people who work in marketing companies. That might seem a little harsh, but these people don't only make the advertisements, they also usually have quite a big say over which television shows get picked up, what movies get made, and how music videos are put together. They might not actually be 'on set', but you won't even get a set unless the marketing types think you can help them sell stuff. In most major television networks around the world the actual programmes are seen pretty much as just the stuff in between the ad breaks. So I think it would be fair-ish to say that when civilization does eventually fall, it will all be the fault of the marketing people.

Unless of course it's the zombies in which case the marketing types are off the hook.

By way of an example, my son plays in a little guys' soccer team, and each week someone gets a Player of the Day certificate which is sponsored by McDonald's. Fair enough, but the certificate also includes a voucher for a free cheeseburger. So after the game we take his voucher down to McDonald's and we get his free cheeseburger, and the rest of us grab something for lunch as well . . . which totals up to close on 25 bucks. As I go to pay, the teenager at the drive-in window says that I can keep the voucher for the free cheeseburger, which I think is a victory for me and for the teenager. She wins because she sneakily lets me keep the voucher, thus striking a small blow against the huge multinational chain that keeps her in servitude; and I win because I can get another free cheeseburger. Of course, 30 seconds after I drive away I suddenly realize what's just happened. The truth is that McDonald's has won, because they've tricked me into coming and spending 25 bucks that I would never have spent unless I'd had that voucher for the $2 cheeseburger — and, what's more, they let me keep it so that I'll come back again and spend another 25 bucks.

So what did I do?

Well, I explained to my son how the clever marketing people at McDonald's had just suckered his old man into spending a whole bunch of money and still making me feel like I'd won, when really I'd been played. Now what we do is we keep the certificates and we bin the vouchers after the following conversation.

Me: Why do they give you this voucher, son?
Him: To trick us into going and spending money.
Me: And are we going to do that?
Him: No.
Me: And why not?
Him: Because we aren't stupid?
Me: That's right, son: because we're not stupid.

This is what you have to do with your daughter whenever you can. For example, imagine you were watching a film with your 10-year-old daughter and the female lead keeps getting into trouble and being rescued by the butch male lead.

You: Why do you think they always show girls needing guys to rescue them?
Her: I don't know.
You: Well, who do you think used to control the movies — boys or girls?
Her: Boys?
You: That's right, so why do you think they might have wanted to make girls look like they couldn't hack it?

Her: Was it to so that boys could say women couldn't do all
the stuff they can?

You: Uh-huh. And so did that make it easier or harder for
girls to get the same jobs as boys?

Her: Harder?

You: That's right. So do you think it's true that boys are
tougher than girls?

Her: No.

You: If you were in a house that was on fire, would you sit
there and scream for some boy to come save you,
or would you get yourself out?

Her: I'd get myself out.

You: Smart girl.

Now, this might sound a little like Feminism 101 to you, and that's because it is. Most blokes don't really stop and consider what the feminists were saying until they actually have a daughter. It's about then that you start becoming acutely aware of how pop culture bullshit — and in fact bullshit in all its many shapes and guises — conspires to keep girls down in all kinds of ways. To be sure, there are now all kinds of other movements like 'girl power' and post-feminism and all sorts of other things, but the basic point remains the same: you need to teach your daughter how to wind her way through the many and varied messages that girls get from everywhere and nowhere that will try to hold her back, or tie her down, or tell her how she should feel, think, or act.

She needs to learn to keep her feet on the ground and not to be suckered by free cheeseburger vouchers. There's no such thing as a free cheeseburger.

When you have a daughter, feminism stops seeming like a good enough idea from a distance — much like combating climate change, or recycling — as you suddenly become aware of all the pop culture horseshit your own daughter gets subjected to.

Then it gets pretty damn personal pretty damn quick.

Tips on
Pop culture bullshit

☆ This stuff is everywhere and nowhere.

☆ You can't shelter her from it, but you can educate her about the inherently bullshit-based nature of some of the worst aspects of popular culture.

☆ Teach her the basics of Feminism 101.

13

The e-girl: raising daughters in the hyper-connected information age

I don't know a dad in the world who doesn't like wandering around an electronics store looking at flat-screen televisions and flash-hot computers. We may not all be IT geeks, but most of us like the toys. I'm sure there are some dads who aren't impressed with a 50" LED flat-screen television, but I've yet to meet one. Similarly, I don't know many dads who would look at a 1-terabyte external hard drive and not be just a little impressed. We don't all know what 1 terabyte is, but we know that whatever it is it's pretty impressive. Oddly, this is a little like being impressed by a really big, empty box — it just seems that much cooler when the box is an electronic one. This fascination with all things techy and cool stands us in good stead when we're trying to come to grips with our kids' online lives.

And trust me, you're going to need to get your head around her online life.

It seems a little odd to think of our kids as having an online life, but they do. It isn't just the websites she's looking at that you need to be worried about; it's also what she's telling the world about herself and who she's talking to. The internet is great in lots of ways, but like the sea it can be both fun and very refreshing, and the next minute can sweep you out of your depth and into the company of nasty creatures with rapacious appetites and well-honed teeth.

It's not even as easy as simply banning the internet from your home, because most schools require kids to have access to the web for assignments; and even if they don't, she'll find internet access in other places. She'll set up a Facebook page while she's at a friend's place and do it that way. They don't call it the World Wide Web for nothing — the bloody thing really is *worldwide*. What I'm going to do here is give you a brief rundown of the major stuff out there that you're going to have to contend with, and some ideas for putting in some checks and balances. The World Wide Web is a fantastic tool that can really enrich our kids' lives if they learn how to make the most of the good stuff . . . and protect themselves from the not-so-good stuff.

And that's where you come in.

Things you can do

The following are my suggestions for some basic precautions you can take to help make the www a safer place for her to be. As with most things, this is a lot easier during the first bit of raising daughters than the second bit. The point here is just the same as in every other aspect of her life: if you do the work during the first bit, and teach her while she actually wants to listen, she's far more likely to make sensible decisions during the second bit.

1 *Keep computers in public places*
  This is fairly common sense, right? If the computer is where you can see it, you can also see what she's doing. Wireless systems can be a problem in this regard, although the solution is pretty simple: just get rid of the wireless and go back to old-fashioned wired access. It's a bad idea for kids to have access to the internet in the privacy of their rooms.

2 *Get to know the services your daughter uses*
It's important that you know which services your daughter uses, and what she can do on those services. The simplest way is to get her to show you. If she takes you on a tour of her internet world, you can see for yourself where she goes, what she does, and the level of savvy she has online.

3 *Use content-filtering software*
There are lots of variations of this stuff out there — everything from software you can buy to internet service providers who offer content filtering as part of their basic service. Remember, though, that she will have access to the online world all over the place, and most of it won't be filtered, so first and foremost your best tool is education.

4 *Teach her that if it sounds too good to be true, it probably is*
I am constantly amazed at how stupid people are when it comes to online scams. Just the other day I received an email with a link stating that it was a survey for McDonald's and that if I answered a few simple questions Ronald McD would give me $50. I was bored, so I opened the link — knowing full well that it was a scam — and clicked a few tick boxes saying how much I thought of this burger and that burger.

At the end of the little questionnaire, it said that if I provided my credit card details, date of birth, address, and driver's licence number, then $50 would be credited into my account.

I typed an obscenity into all the boxes.

5 *Teach her that people may not be who they say they are*
Again it's pretty obvious, but it still needs to be said. Sometimes she might be talking to a nine-year-old girl called Phoebe, and sometimes Phoebe could really be a 49-year-old sex offender whose real name is Brian.

6 *Most of all, teach her never to give out any personal information*
— ever

This one is the most important message of all to make sure
that she understands. An alarming number of kids will tell
complete strangers, like 'Phoebe', all kinds of things about
themselves — where they go to school, where they live,
and a whole pile of other stuff as well. She needs to really
understand why it's important that she never gives out any
personal information. Ever.

7 *Set rules for computer use*

As with any activity, our job as parents is to define
reasonable limits and educate our kids, including how to
navigate the online world safely.

Rules for online safety

It's a very good idea to make sure that you and your daughter
have some basic rules around online safety. These should be
clearly explained, and she should understand why these rules
are important. The New Zealand Department of Internal Affairs
recommends that the following rules (based on material from the
National Centre for Missing and Exploited Children in Arlington
Virginia in the United States) should be printed out, signed, and
put up on the wall by the computer.

1. I will not give out personal information such as my address,
   telephone number, parents' work address/telephone number,
   or the name and location of my school without my parents'
   permission.

2. I will tell my parents right away if I come across any
   information that makes me feel uncomfortable.

3. I will never agree to get together with someone I 'meet'
   online without first checking with my parents. If my parents

agree to the meeting, I will be sure that it is in a public place and bring my mother or father along.

4. I will never send a person my picture or anything else without first checking with my parents.

5. I will not respond to any messages that are mean or in any way make me feel uncomfortable. It is not my fault if I get a message like that. If I do, I will tell my parents right away so that they can contact the online service.

6. I will talk with my parents so that we can set up rules for going online. We will decide upon the time of day that I can be online, the length of time I can be online, and appropriate areas for me to visit. I will not access other areas or break these rules without their permission.

Dolphins online

The Hector's dolphin is one of the smallest of the dolphins, weighing in at something like 50 kilograms and measuring only about 1.2–1.6 metres long. There aren't many of them left either; best guess is something just over 7,000, with one of the largest populations being in Akaroa Harbour in Canterbury, New Zealand. If you YouTube the Hector's dolphin, you'll see that they are very fine little dolphins indeed, but this isn't what makes them remarkable.

No, the really remarkable thing is that the Hector's dolphin is the only cetacean to use the internet to better its chances of not being killed by people. It seems that this humble, but very PR-savvy, little dolphin has set up its own interactive website, www.hectorsworld.com, aimed at teachings kids and their parents about online safety. Incredibly, these canny little marine mammals have decided that the best way to survive is to help kids in the hope that it will make us parents want to kill Hector's dolphins less.

There are lots of great resources on their site to teach kids how to wander around the web and keep themselves safe. There's also lots of information for parents which can help you think about how you can help your daughter to figure out all this online safety stuff. Another quite clever little freebie on the site is a free button (a little cartoon Hector's dolphin) you can download which sits on the top of your screen, and, if your kids ever end up in a website with upsetting content, they just click the button and the screen fills with nice underwater scenes so they don't have to look at the bad stuff and can come get you.

So, I don't know about you, but since the Hector's dolphins have gone to all this trouble to make such a great resource to educate me and my kids about online safety, then given the choice I think next time I'll kill a different species of dolphin rather than the Hector's . . . like say a bottlenose dolphin. I mean, what have those selfish sods ever done for anyone but themselves?

Screw them, I say.

Little kids' virtual worlds

If you don't already know about virtual worlds, then you should probably get yourself acquainted with them. In some ways the whole virtual world phenomenon is a bit sad, yet at the same time it's a bit cool as well. How many things in life can pull off being both sad and cool, and still make sense? The sad part comes from the fact that, instead of having an actual real life, people go online and spend hours and hours putting time and effort into something that doesn't really exist; the cool part comes from the fact that many of these virtual worlds are pretty cool.

The biggest adult virtual world in the world is a place called Second Life, which, for many people, really is a second life. Essentially it's a 3D world where you can have a whole other life, and what's more you can fly. There are over a million people who've signed up for a Second Life, and many of them own property, sell products, have feuds, fall in love, and do just about everything that people do out here for real; just in there, it's all virtual. You might be inclined to dismiss this stuff as geeky nonsense but that might be a mistake, because big corporations and even some universities are setting up shop there as well. In fact there's a thing called Second Life Grid, where businesses, educational bodies, and people who want to work in a virtual world can log in and get real stuff done. Large corporations like Xerox and IBM have Second Life conferences rather than flying everyone around the world to actual conferences.

But it isn't just the huge multinationals — it's our kids as well. There are online virtual worlds for children, too, and a weird little place called Club Penguin is probably the biggest player in the field at the moment. In this cartoon virtual world, kids can have their own penguin persona, or avatar, and can decorate their own igloo, play games, and have virtual pets. You might think this is mere child's play, but Disney bought Club Penguin in 2007 for $700 million.

Clearly the suits think that there is big money to be made, mostly through the membership fees the kids pay if they want more than the basic service, and for the sale of virtual knick-knacks to fancy up their virtual selves. For parents, the nice thing about Club Penguin is that it's a very safe place for kids to play online, because there are tight restrictions on the kinds of information that kids are able to divulge.

Which makes it a good place to start learning about having a safe online life.

Social-networking sites

It's practically inevitable that your girl will end up having her own page on Facebook or Bebo, and there's an increasing likelihood that she may tweet on Twitter as well. Social networking is one of the big winners of the internet, with Facebook alone having over

250 million registered users and an estimated value of anywhere from $2.7 to $5 billion. How it works, if you don't know, is that you sign up and receive what is effectively a free personal web page where you can post information about yourself, including photographs, and people can click on links to become your 'friends' so they can see your updates, and send you messages.

Sounds great, huh? It is a great way to stay in touch with people, especially people that you don't see every day, or family living overseas, or even complete strangers who become your online 'friends'. The problem for many kids is that they don't stop to think about the fact that anything they put on their Facebook page will be visible to any Tom, Dick or 'Phoebe' who clicks on asking to be their friend.

As with all this stuff, it's about trying to educate your kids to think about what they are posting on their page, and the possible ramifications of that further on down the road. Some employers, for example, will search potential employees' Facebook pages to see what they can learn. If your girl has posted pictures of her and her friends partying up large, or even more compromising information, it might cost her a job.

But hang on: does that mean that I can log on to Facebook under a pseudonym and then ask to be her Facebook 'friend' so that I can get the inside scoop on what's going on in her life?

Yes, I suppose you can.

Would that be wrong? I mean, it's a little like spying, which does seem kind of wrong — but then it would be one way to keep track of what she's up to.

I couldn't possibly say.

'Couldn't possibly say' because you think it's wrong, or 'couldn't possibly say' because you don't want to be seen to be condoning sneaky tactics?

I couldn't possibly say.

Mobile phones

Like me, you can probably remember when the only people who had mobile phones were yuppie posers, and the phones themselves were as big as bricks. Now they're tiny, amazing, and everywhere. Inevitably, the question arises as to when you should let your kids own a mobile phone . . . and usually the question is first raised by your kids. Sadly, many of them think that if they simply keep raising the question every 23.4 seconds, then you'll give in and let them have one.

As with many things in life and parenting, there is no absolute right answer on this one. There's no scientifically proven formula for deciding when kids should have a phone, so it's pretty much going to come down to whenever you think is best. For what it's worth, here's my take on the issue.

◊ The reason you get her a phone is to make it easier for you to stay in touch with her when she's out there in the world by herself. For that reason, I don't see why anyone younger than say 12 or 13 would actually need one.

◊ It might be that your daughter is involved in a lot of sports or other activities where you need to co-ordinate pickup times, etc, with her, in which case it's possible she might need one a little younger than that.

◊ If the only reason she wants one is so that she can send text messages to her friends, then I'd make her wait. Frankly, I think it's kind of silly that eight- and nine-year-olds have mobile phones.

◊ When you do get her a phone, think carefully about why you want her to have it. If the predominant reason is simply to make it easier to contact her, then she doesn't need one that will also let her access the internet. If she can surf the web from her phone, your ability to monitor what she does online all but disappears.

The other upside of mobile phones, quite aside from the ability to communicate with her, is that it also gives you something you can take away from her when you're looking for something to punish her with. Still, we'll get to that later on in Chapter 17.

Tips on
The e-Girl

☆ Keep computers in public places.

☆ Get to know the sites and services she uses.

☆ Use content-filtering software.

☆ Teach her that if it sounds too good to be true, it probably is.

☆ Teach her never to give out personal information.

☆ Set rules for computer use.

☆ Educate yourself about all this IT stuff and monitor it as best you can.

14

Puberty
— it's not as scary as it seems

OK, so the title of this chapter was just a cheap trick to get you to read it. Puberty *is* scary; in fact for many fathers raising daughters, this is the bit where you are most likely to want to run as far and as fast as your legs can carry you. If you're raising her with her mum, then you can shuffle off somewhere for a lot of this stuff, and truth be told she's probably far more comfortable talking about it with her mum than with you. If mum isn't there, though, or if you're separated and she spends time with her mum and time with you, then you're going to have to get your head around all this stuff.

So what we're going to do in this chapter is go through the whole thing in almost agonizing detail. Most of us have a general idea of what the whole 'women stuff' is about. Truth be told, most of us know enough to know that we don't want to know too much. Some things should remain a mystery. Sadly, as with many things, if you're raising a girl then you don't have the luxury of having only a slight awareness of the issues. You are going to need to know the nitty-gritty, and all the supporting information that goes with the nitty-gritty. Steel yourself, men, because we're going to talk about mucous, and secretions, and 'feminine products'.

The reason for this is not just that you should probably know all about that stuff, but also if you have buckets of technical information you can focus on that when you're talking with her about 'girly stuff'. Most fathers will probably find it easier to focus on the technical details than the actual reality of what you're talking to her about.

It is, after all, just plumbing.

We're not going to talk all that much about the psychological aspects of teenagers in this chapter. For now I'm just going to focus on the hardware, not the software. This is the nuts and bolts of puberty. It's the anatomy and physiology of 'girly stuff'. We'll get to all the rest of it in the next chapter.

You can actually slow it all down

It is one of the truly amazing things of fatherhood that just your presence in the home can slow down the onset of puberty for girls. Crazy, but true. There are now a number of quite large-scale studies that have found that girls whose fathers lived in the house began puberty later than girls whose fathers were absent. Except it was a little more complex than that, in that it wasn't so much just the presence of a father in the house but also the quality of the parents' relationship with each other that really counted. The better mum and dad got on, the later the daughter entered puberty.

So if you're around, and you make sure that your daughter(s) see you and their mum have a warm, loving relationship, then you can potentially have a real impact on prolonging her childhood.

Having said that, it is speeding up all by itself

If you were raising a girl in the 19th century, she would have had her first period on average at about age 17. By 1960, the year that John F Kennedy announced his candidacy for the Democratic presidential nomination, and also the year when Elvis Presley returned home after three years' military service in Germany, the average age of the onset of puberty had dropped to 12–13 years. Now Elvis is dead, and the average age of onset of puberty is 10 years for girls and 11.5 years for boys. As an average, girls tend to begin their periods around age 12, but the other changes of puberty can begin much younger.

There are all kinds of possible, and complicated, explanations for why that might be. It's likely that better nutrition is playing a big role, but it could also be that childhood obesity is a bigger issue now, as well as the fact that children are exposed to more chemicals and nasty stuff.

Ultimately none of that stuff matters to you, because the 'why' isn't anywhere as important as the 'when', and the when is without question a lot earlier than it ever used to be.

The miracle of puberty

When you actually stop and think about what happens during puberty, it is pretty bloody amazing. Through a complicated process that involves her 'biological clock' and internal chemical feedback mechanisms, her body decides that it's time to get ready to make babies. So somewhere between the ages of 8 and 13-ish the pituitary gland in the brain secretes follicle-stimulating hormone (FSH) into the bloodstream, which travels down to ovaries and stimulates the production of oestrogen.

Now, I know that FSH is actually a 'hormone', but in my mind's eye I always imagine this as a bit like a bunch of 'sassy chicks' in a Cadillac cruising down through the great spaghetti junction of the circulatory system with loud music blaring on the stereo, long hair blowing in the wind, and laughing their arses off. It's basically the greatest biological road trip in the world as the FSHs get on down to get the business done.

There's a revolution comin', baby.

Girl power's on the move, and she ain't takin' no prisoners. As soon as the FSH hits the ovaries, then oestrogen production goes into full swing, and from that point there's no turning back. Childhood is left behind in a cloud of swirling hormones as the body prepares itself to make babies. That's a scary thought, I know, but the end goal of all that is going to happen over the next few years: the propagation of the species.

The stages of puberty

The first noticeable sign of puberty in girls is breast development. This can begin as young as 8 years but on average starts at around age 10, and is first evident as a swelling or 'budding' around the nipple. This can be the start of an anxious time for girls, because they can worry about how they look and can also get teased sometimes, particularly if they start to develop earlier (or later) than their peers. Clearly this means that you're going to have to be talking to her about all this so you can know if she's having problems. We'll get to the how you do that in a moment, but just for now it's important to know that for girls these first obvious signs of puberty can be a time of awkwardness or self-consciousness.

The next step is developing pubic hair and underarm hair. Generally pubic hair begins to develop roughly between the ages of 9 and 15, with underarm hair following along about two years after the first signs of pubic hair. This is also the time that girls first start waxing or shaving their legs, because that stuff also begins to get a lot more noticeable around that time as well.

The other changes that accompany all the hormonal ups and downs are weight gain and pimples. The reason that women gain weight during this time is to prepare their bodies for having children, which is why they gain weight in their breasts, hips and thighs. Just as with boys, there will be growth spurts during adolescence, with most people reaching their full adult height somewhere between 15 and 19. The pimples come from hormonally-based changes in the oiliness of their skin.

I know what you're thinking here.

What? What was I thinking?

You're thinking: Yeah, but what about that other thing?

What do you mean?

The M-word.

Oh.

The M-word

Menstruation.

There, we said it. Not so bad, is it?

This is pretty much Ground Zero for paternal discomfort when it comes to daughters. Mostly this part of the feminine world is a bit of a mystery to most blokes. We might understand the basics, but not many of us want to know anything more than the absolute necessities in this regard. Not so you: you need to know all about it. So what I'm going to do here is first explain the plumbing, and then get onto the hardware.

And actually, once you start thinking about it like plumbing — like a series of connected systems which all have a job to do — then it isn't quite as scary to think about as it might first seem. I'm going to get quite technical here, though, because if you're anything like me there is something oddly comforting in the technical details.

As a ballpark average, menstruation starts sometime around 12 years of age, roughly two years after breast development begins. You have to remember that these are simply averages; for some girls the process may begin earlier, and for some a little later. Because this is usually a big deal for most girls, it's important that you understand what's going on so you feel confident talking to her about what's happening if the situation demands.

The menstrual cycle (which sounds like something a clown

would ride whilst telling dirty jokes) is divided up into three distinct phases: menstruation (that's the bit commonly called 'the period'), the follicular phase, and the luteal phase. Ovulation, which is when the egg or ovum is released, marks the transition from the follicular phase to the luteal phase. The length of the menstrual cycles will vary from woman to woman, and from cycle to cycle, but 28 days is the average, and the first day of menstruation, when her period begins, is counted as Day 1.

For most guys the fact there are three separate phases is a bit of a surprise. Most think that there's pretty much just the messy bit, and then the other bits and bobs sit around playing Pacman the rest of the time. Actually that couldn't be further from the truth, because the female reproductive system is a pretty amazing piece of machinery. Here's how the whole thing works in sequence, starting at Day 1 of the menstrual cycle.

1 Menstruation is the part of the cycle where there is some bleeding. We'll get to why at the other end of the cycle, but just for now let's just stick with bleeding happens on Day 1. This can last anywhere from two to seven days and usually involves the loss of anywhere between 10 and 80 millimetres of blood. The reason that the blood flow continues is because an enzyme called *plasmin* inhibits clotting to effectively 'flush out' the system (see, told you it was basically plumbing). This part of the cycle can also be accompanied by cramps in the abdomen, back, or upper thighs. This is also obviously the point where tampons and pads are necessary, and we'll cover off the hardware options below as well.

2 During the first few days of the cycle, our old friends the FSHs (follicle stimulating hormones) are released, which stimulate the ovarian follicles to grow. This is actually a competitive process under the influence of several different hormones. Just like that fantastic film

Highlander, there can be only one, and so it is with the ovarian follicles, with only one maturing into an ovum or egg. Unlike *Highlander*, there's no actual sword-fighting involved, which, given the lack of space, is probably just as well.

3 The developing follicles secrete both *oestradiol* and *oestrogen*, which in turn stimulate a thickening of the *endometrium*, which is the technical name for the wall of the *uterus*. The *oestrogen* also stimulates the *cervix* to produce cervical mucus. This sounds pretty gross, but the cervical mucus is important in reproduction because it essentially provides a ladder for the sperm to travel up the uterus into the fallopian tubes to fertilize the egg or ovum.

4 As the follicles are developing, the amount of *oestradiol* they produce gradually increases until it reaches a trigger level, which then sets off production of *luteinizing hormone* (LH), usually somewhere around Day 12 of the cycle. This hormone helps complete the final stages of preparing the egg and its eventual release into the *fallopian tube*.

5 The egg is swept from the ovary into the fallopian tube by a small fringe of tissue called *fimbriae*.

6 After about a day, if the egg is not fertilized (which all fathers pray for) it dissolves. Phew.

7 The next bit it is called the *luteal phase*. After the egg is released, a part of the ovary called the *corpus luteum* continues to grow and produces a number of hormones, but one in particular called *progesterone*. This hormone is like the ground crew of an aircraft carrier, because its job is to make the deck of the uterus ready for the fertilized egg to land on. Cunningly, if the egg isn't fertilized the corpus luteum also suppresses production of the hormones it needs to keep going — FSH and LH — and so it essentially shrivels up.

8 This triggers the onset of menstruation, or 'the period', as the uterus walls break down, resulting in a small amount of bleeding, which brings us all the way back to Day 1 again.

See what I mean about how all that stuff is both complex and busy? Just to be sure, here's all that complicated stuff in one simple little diagram. This gives the major events and a guide to when, *on average*, each phase or event should be occurring.

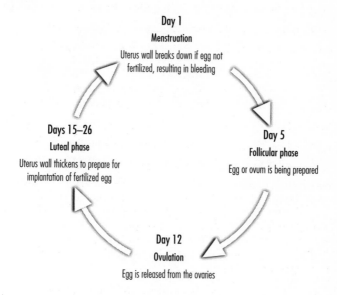

Day 1

Menstruation

Uterus wall breaks down if egg not fertilized, resulting in bleeding

Day 5

Follicular phase

Egg or ovum is being prepared

Day 12

Ovulation

Egg is released from the ovaries

Days 15–26

Luteal phase

Uterus wall thickens to prepare for implantation of fertilized egg

The Hardware

Your basic options here are sanitary pads and tampons. For the vast majority of girls tampons seem like a pretty big jump to begin with, so most usually start with pads. These look a little like sterile bandages, and some even have wings, and they are placed inside the underwear to soak up blood during the period. They need to be changed every couple of hours, depending on the volume of flow. Pads are generally the easiest, lowest-tech, lowest-anxiety method of managing that 'time of the month'. Most girls start with pads because they seem easier to begin with.

Tampons are made of soft cotton and are inserted inside the vagina to absorb the menstrual flow. They look a little like a large cotton bud with a string attached, kind of like a little cotton mouse. Girls usually have all kind of questions about tampons, and the internet can be a great aid here. There are lots and lots of sites that offer all kinds of useful advice and assistance about choosing and using tampons. Just google it and you'll find all the information about 'feminine needs' that you could ever want.

PMS

Whatever you do, tread carefully here, because this one is a bit of a nightmare all round. Sometimes just the suggestion of PMS (premenstrual syndrome) can bring on a dose of ABYSIHPMSS (angry because you said I had premenstrual syndrome syndrome). Essentially you can't win any way with this one, so best just try to understand a little of what it is. Usually the symptoms occur during the two weeks prior to the period beginning, and usually disappear either just before or just after the start of the menstrual flow. Symptoms of PMS include the following:

◇ bloating

◇ cramps

◇ breast tenderness

◇ stress/anxiety

◇ muscle pain

◇ insomnia

◇ headache

◇ fatigue

◇ acne

◇ mood swings

◇ irritability

◇ cataclysmic metamorphosis into evil she-demon.

No one really knows what causes PMS at the moment. It seems to occur in the luteal phase of the menstrual cycle, although most sufferers seem to have normal levels of the various sex hormones — so all round it's a bit of a mystery. Best guess would seem to be that the hormones somehow affect brain chemistry. Who knows, and who cares really? All you need to know is how to survive it. The trick would seem to be to understand that, like Buddha said, life is suffering, and that this suffering may regularly intensify as people in your house progress through the luteal phase. Expect it, roll with it, live through it. If things are particularly bad, you may want to think about consulting your family doctor to see if she can help.

How to talk about all this stuff

It's pretty clear that there's a lot going on for girls during puberty, so it's important that you start talking about it as early as seems appropriate.

See, now straight away I know what you're thinking — you're thinking: *Yeah, easy for you to say that, smart guy, you've got two boys. How the hell do I start talking to my daughter about that stuff?*

I have no qualms in admitting that I feel a vast amount of relief that I have two boys when it comes to all this stuff. There's no escaping the fact that it's harder if you're a dad raising daughters when it comes to puberty, and especially talking about puberty. So I sympathize with your plight, truly, but it really is *your* plight. She only has one dad, and that's you, so this is one of those times you have to stop whining and get on with it.

Probably the best way to think about all this is to forget all the *sexual* weirdness and just concentrate on the mechanics of it. This is really just a great big plumbing issue when you break it down, so if you focus on the physical/technical aspects of it, then you'll probably find yourself having an easier time of it.

This would be one example of how such a conversation might go.

You: So you know how you're nearly 11 now?
Her: Yeah.
You: I was wondering if you had any questions about what puberty is, and how your body changes as you get older.
Her: *Dad!* . . . No.
You: OK, but if you do you can just ask me. Part of my job is to help you to understand all of that stuff.
Her: *Dad!*
You: I'm just saying.

Three weeks later . . .

You: Did you read that book I left on your bed?
Her: Uh, yep.
You: And what did you think of it?
Her: It was alright, I guess.
You: Did you have any questions about any of it?
Her: I don't know.
You: It's really important that you understand all the changes that are going on for you right now, and most of all you need to know you can ask me about any of that stuff. Some of it can seem a little confusing at first, like when periods start and all that, so it's important that you know you can talk to me about it at any time. I know about all that — even about oestrogen and plasmin.
Her: What's that?

You: Oestrogen is like a chemical in a girl's body that helps prepare her for the first part of her menstrual cycle, and plasmin is another type of chemical called an enzyme which helps to control how long a period lasts.

Her: How does it do that?

You: What? The oestrogen or the plasmin?

Her: The 'plas-whatever'.

And just like that, you're off and talking.

There are a hundred ways into the conversation, but if you start off with the technical bits then it might seem a little more 'functional' and a little less weird. Plus, if you have technical stuff to talk about, you don't need to worry about what to say. Just explain the actual process in as simple or as complicated a way as works for the two of you.

The big thing here is that you simply need to talk about it. This isn't a 'one big talk' and then you can cross it off the list kind of thing. This is a conversation that will need to be revisited from time to time either when she brings it up, or when you think there are things that need to be talked about.

Reinforcements

It's likely that, even if you do arm yourself with knowledge, diagrams, and props, there are still going to be times she might need to go and talk to a fellow girl about girl-stuff. If that's the case, there are a number of places you can go for reinforcements:

◊ a friendly female family doctor

◊ aunts and grandmothers

◊ books written by women for girls (such as *The Puberty Book: Everything You Don't Want to Ask But Need to Know*, which is available on Amazon.com)

◇ the mother of one of her friends

◇ older female cousins

◇ Family Planning Clinics.

All these people and places are usually good sources of help and support for both daughters and dads going it alone.

Tips on
Puberty

☆ The average age for the onset of puberty in girls is around 10 years.

☆ Puberty might seem pretty scary, but if you get familiar with the technical details it all gets easier to talk about.

☆ Remember: basically you're just talking about a very sophisticated plumbing system.

☆ This isn't something you do once and cross off the list — she will need to revisit it from time to time as different issues crop up.

☆ Get educated about the whole thing and you should be fine.

15

Adolescence — the place where 'dad jokes' go to die

I was talking to a friend of mine the other day and he was saying that lately he'd noticed that dad jokes no longer worked with his 10-year-old daughter; in fact, quite the opposite. Where once the deft use of dad jokes could cajole and jolly her along to get done whatever needed to be done, now they just seemed to make her mad.

'It's a qualitative shift,' he said. 'It isn't simply that she's gotten a little older and a little smarter, so we need to adjust our response a little — it's like there's a whole new push for control. I can see her wanting to really control what she does and doesn't do in a way that's very different. And now I find myself thinking of what's potentially coming in the next few years, and I'm leaning a little more towards wanting to control her more than I ever have before.'

Eventually all dad jokes die. For those first few years, every dad is a successful comedian. We tell our crap jokes, and make our stupid wisecracks, and they always get a laugh. Sometimes our kids laugh so hard that they literally fall off things, which is deeply satisfying for most dads; but sooner or later the crowd changes, they mature, and what used to be funny is funny no more.

Suddenly you're not the guy who packs out concert halls for

every gig, suddenly you're the sad old bugger with thinning hair and a pot belly who struggles to get gigs at the local golf club. No one thinks you're funny anymore, and that stings, because you can remember when you had them rolling in the bloody aisles.

It's quite common for many dads to become a little dispirited at this stage, and it's also quite common for dads to feel like the best thing they can do is simply to retire from the comedy circuit and get off the stage. There's only so much heckling a guy can take, only so many booing crowds and empty seats. At some point it's all going to get too much, and that's when you're going to ask yourself whether it's time to quit, time to retire from the circuit and go find a shed somewhere to hide in.

What kills dad jokes?

The ugly truth is that it's biology that kills dad jokes, and most likely it has a lot to do with some stuff called gonadotropin-releasing hormone (GnRH). It's this stuff that gets released from a structure deep in the brain once a very complicated biological clock decides that it's time to get busy with all the stuff we talked about in the previous chapter, and with it comes the inevitable death of 'dad jokes'. The swirly-whirly of adolescence sometimes sucks the life from dad humour and creates an air of sulky frustration too dense to support life. At the point where puberty kicks in, so too does adolescence, which is the psychological/ behavioural part of growing up.

Somewhere in that complex dance of biology and psychology, dad jokes simply run out of oxygen. They don't satisfy her anymore; she will not be cajoled or jollied along into things. Now she is starting to get some idea that life really is out there waiting for her, and she won't be fobbed off or distracted.

Where once you might have been able to make some wisecrack to muddle through, you suddenly discover she won't settle for that anymore. She wants more: even though most of the time she might not know what she wants more of, she just knows she wants more of it.

You see, not only is her body changing, but her brain is changing, too, and with that her very self is changing. It isn't only her physical shape that changes to accommodate her new adultness, it's her psychological shape as well. She must begin to get her head around the fact that she is no longer a little kid, and that the rules have changed forever.

And so must you.

All of which is why you might suddenly find that the stuff which used to make her laugh now just makes her mad. When she was a child, she was content to be handled, to be managed; but now that the adult world is knocking on the door, she simply can't do that anymore. She might not want to move out and get her own apartment in the city just yet, but she's going to be feeling like all that corny little kid stuff is ever so slightly tired.

Maturity isn't a straight-line thing

The point which many parents get wrong is that, because their kids are looking more and more like adults, they expect them to act more and more like adults. Whilst that might be true for brief, and sometimes startlingly insightful moments, it isn't true all the time.

Maturity isn't something that happens like some straight line on a graph. Instead, it's a bit more like climbing through the Andes Mountains, with the journey marked by soaring peaks, jaw-dropping precipices, and often near-vertical drop-offs into valley floors thousands of feet below. You must be careful where you tread here, because what looks like solid ground might slip away beneath your feet in a moment.

And as you tumble end-over-end, wondering when you'll hit the ground, you always feel equal measures of surprise, disappointment, and usually abject terror.

The teenage brain

If you have a teenager, you might find yourself wondering at times what happened to the previously fairly functional brain that had got her through most of her childhood. Apart from the odd glitch, you might have thought that her brain was in quite good working order, and had seemed to rattle along in a reasonably logical fashion. Then, for no apparent reason, it seems to lose its own mind.

We've all probably heard of the importance of the first three years of life for brain development, but it's only in the past few years that researchers have started to get a better handle on the fact that the teenage years are also a time of great development and change. Just as the complex biology of puberty bathes the body in hormones which trigger physical development and maturation in her body, it also marks a time of fairly substantial changes in her brain.

Grey matter and white matter — the only matter that matters

You might have heard the term 'grey matter' before, and you also might have heard of 'white matter'. These terms refer to how different parts of brain cells — or *neurons* — appear on brain scans. It's a long way from imaginative, but essentially the main body of the neuron or brain cell appears grey in a brain scan, and the fatty insulation — called *myelin* — around the connections which sprout off from the body of the neuron show up as white.

Grey matter and white matter. I guess they came up with such boring names because brains are so bloody interesting that they had far more important things on their minds than coming up with cool names. Still, it's a bit of shame they couldn't have put just a little more thought into it so at least it would have been cooler for the rest of us who aren't automatically fascinated by brain research.

One of those interesting things is that — boring name

notwithstanding — the grey matter in various parts of the brain peaks in volume around a year or two earlier in girls than in boys. This may help explain why girls in their early teens tend to find boys of the same age slightly immature and a bit silly. Now, having said that, you always need to keep in mind that care must be taken in deducing too much from *any* observed differences in boys' and girls' brains. Not only is there a lot of individual variation between both boys and girls, but it's also quite difficult to say what a size difference in the brain makes to behaviour in the real world. So, it's interesting, but we're a long way from knowing anything definitive about what those differences mean.

What's also interesting, while we're on the subject of interesting things, is that the development of white matter increases fairly steadily throughout childhood and adolescence. The white matter acts as an insulator by wrapping the branches of the neurons in a fatty layer. This helps speed the transmission of nerve impulses, a little like insulation around a cable.

What has only recently been discovered, though, is that not only does the white matter increase the speed of transmission of nerve impulses, but it also regulates the timing and synchronicity of those impulses as well.

So as they age, there seems to be an ever-increasing efficiency in the speed and timing of nerve impulses. You may not get wiser as you get older, but you certainly develop a system which starts to work more efficiently with age.

Those all-important frontal lobes

For most of us, the brain is simply a great grey wrinkly blob, but for your average neuroscientist the brain is actually a dizzyingly fascinating collection of separate but connected systems which in some mad, hideously complex, and yet to be fully understood way all work together to make us who we are. Now, whilst they're all obviously pretty important, one of the more significant parts of the brain is the *frontal lobe*. It will probably come as no surprise to you, given the poor form neuroscientists have shown in naming things thus far, that the frontal lobe is the front bit of the brain. It turns out the frontal lobe is very important in higher brain functions, like risk appraisal and planning.

One piece of this part of the brain is very important indeed, and is called the *prefrontal cortex*. This part of the brain is so important that, in a rare burst of metaphorical fancy, some neuroscientists have called it the 'seat of reason'. The prefrontal cortex is the part of our brains that is fundamental to a number of important tasks, one of which is the evaluation of risk.

It's a little like if the rest of your brain is telling you to do something it all turns to the prefrontal cortex for the final approval. Not only that, but the prefrontal cortex is also the bit that tends to tell the rest of your brain to chill out when you're getting wound up.

Add to that all the important social roles it plays (like self-awareness and allowing you to understand other people's perspectives), and you get some idea of how important this little wrinkly sub-blob is.

What we now know is that neuron (the technical name for a brain cell) growth peaks in the frontal lobe at around 11 years of age in girls and 12.1 years of age in boys. You might draw some immediate comfort from that, because you could be forgiven for thinking that this is automatically a good thing. Surely if growth peaks in that area at age 11, then your daughter is going to be well-prepared to make really good decisions about what's risky and what isn't, right?

Sadly, no.

To understand why that is, you need to know a little something about how the teenage brain essentially expands and shrinks over only a few short years, and more specifically why the shrinking is a good thing.

Too much of a good thing: the incredible expanding-shrinking teenage brain

As we saw in the previous chapter on puberty, the human body is a truly amazing thing, and that is doubly true for the brain. You've probably heard all about how the first three years of life are a 'critical period' for children's brain development, but not as many people have heard about how important the teenage years are as well.

Just as there is a proliferation on brain development in the first three years, there is a second brain 'growth spurt' during adolescence, which is why we see the peak in grey matter growth at around age 11 in girls.

The problem is that, as with salt, too much of anything hardly ever works out for the best. So it is with grey matter. As one concrete example, researchers have found that when children were asked to match pictures of a face displaying particular facial expressions with words describing those expressions (eg, happy, sad, angry), there was actually a *deterioration* in performance at the start of puberty.

Children and older adolescents were better at matching facial expressions to words describing those emotions.

Why would that be?

The best theory at the moment seems to be that it really is a matter of too much of a good thing. Neurons are great, but it seems that the proliferation of neurons at the start of puberty effectively clogs up the system, and means they can't do some tasks as well as when they had a little more headspace. The reason that older adolescents are better at these types of tasks is that — just as in the brains of very young children who are similarly clogged with neurons and connections — there is a pruning of the excess wiring, a gradual decline in the amount of grey matter as some connections are kept and some are discarded; like old newspapers, they simply disappear into the gutters and back alleys of the teenage brain.

Teenage risk-taking is really all about back-seat driving

If you cast your own mind back to your teenage years, there were probably one or two things you did which, in hindsight, were pretty bloody silly. You wouldn't be alone there; I've got one or two things I did as a teenager which make me go a bit pale now when I think about them. Once when I was teenager, just as a brief example by way of self-confession, I went abseiling with a friend. We both sort of knew what we were doing, but I was a bit rusty on the whole knot-tying front. So I tied a kind of triple granny knot, and off over the edge of a hundred-foot cliff we both went. At the time it seemed all very reasonable. Looking back on it now, I think I'd want to be pretty certain that the knot was an official abseiling knot that had been approved by far smarter people than me.

'You can tell from their eyes'

I once was asked to try to talk some sense into a 14-year-old girl who was running away all the time. She lived in a semi-rural area that was bordered by one of the roughest neighbourhoods in the city. Ashly had developed the completely alarming practice of climbing out her bedroom window in the early hours of the morning and walking for miles down isolated country roads to meet up with her friends. In fact the week before I saw her, a girl's body had been found dumped on the side of the road in the same area. This young woman had been killed by her psychopathic ex-boyfriend and simply left in a ditch.

'Did you hear about the girl who was murdered last week?' I asked her.

'Yeah.'

'Does that worry you?'

She frowned at me as if I'd just asked the stupidest question in the history of questions. 'No.'

'Why not?'

'I can take care of myself.'

Despite the dire seriousness of the conversation, I couldn't help myself from laughing. She was a tiny slip of a thing, and about as streetwise as a wet flannel. 'You what?'

'I can take care of myself.'

'How do you figure that, then?'

'Because I can tell who's bad and who isn't.'

'Really?'

'Yeah.'

'How do you do that then?'

'Their eyes,' she said, in a tone that suggested she was sharing one of the great secrets of life on the streets.

'Their eyes?'

'Yeah.'

'What about their eyes?'

'I dunno, you can just tell.'

'From their eyes?'

She nodded sagely.

'How many murderers have you met?' I asked her.

'None.'

'Oh, so you've never actually met an actual murderer?'

'No.'

'Do you know how many I've met?'

'How many?'

'Lots. When I'm not talking to teenagers, I spend the rest of my time talking to murderers and rapists, and drug dealers — all kinds of bad guys.'

'Really?' She finally seemed interested.

'Really. And some of them looked just like you'd expect a murderer to look, with the crazy eyes and the prison tattoos and all that shit, but some of them looked just the opposite. Some of them looked like the nicest guys you could ever hope to meet. They were polite, and courteous, and had a really great sense of humour.'

'For real?'

'For real. And do you know the only way that I could tell that these nice, polite, courteous, charming guys were killers?'

'How?'

'I read their file.'

'What did it say?'

I sighed. 'That's not the point. The point is that you can't always tell who the bad guys are, because they sometimes look just like the nice guys. And do you know what else?'

'What?'

'Girls like you are the perfect target for bad guys like that. He'd be charming and polite and offer you a ride — and by the time you figured out you were in real trouble, it would be way too late.'

We sat there for a moment in silence. I wondered if she'd taken in any of what I'd said.

'Well it doesn't matter anyway,' she said at last.

'Why?'

'We did a self-defence class at school.'

And the scariest thing about our whole conversation was that she actually believed that.

So why do teenagers take such crazy risks?

It would be easy to simply characterize them as being a bit dizzy or unthinking, but that's actually quite a long way from the truth. It seems that there's some pretty good evidence that the teenage brain develops in a way that's slightly out of kilter, and this predisposes them to making what seem at face value to be slightly mad decisions. There is now quite good evidence which seems to show that teenagers engage in risky and dangerous activities *despite* the fact that they understand full well the risks involved. While they might know something is dangerous, they are more influenced by their *feelings* and their *friends*.

Once puberty kicks in, there are changes in the stimulus-reward centres in the deeper levels of the brain which almost propel the teenager towards thrill-seeking. Unfortunately, the part of the brain which is supposed to keep all this stuff in check, our old friend the prefrontal cortex, is still getting itself sorted out. The end result is that the engine is revving up but the driver is not quite all there. If they are alone and they have plenty of time to think about it, then they are able to make fairly sensible decisions; but when you add in friends and even the faintest whiff of a 'buzz', all bets are off.

Mad Aunty Harriet

The simplest way to think about all this stuff is to keep in mind Mad Aunty Harriet. Imagine for a moment that your extended family have had a meeting and decided that Mad Aunty Harriet must come and live with you. She had spent many years living fairly happily in a private institution for the 'somewhat unhinged', but — following a scandal involving illegal turtle-racing and some fairly significant accounting irregularities — the place was closed down. What's more, because you never actually went to the family meeting everyone has voted in your absence that she live with you.

Bugger.

Not much you can do, though, and so in she moves, albeit to a cot in the basement. Imagine further, that one night you're watching television and you ask Mad Aunty H if she'd like a cup of tea. At this point she leaps to her feet, bursts into tears, calls you a 'fucking bastarding shit-heel bastard' and storms off to the basement.

Would you be upset?

Probably not, would be my guess. I'd imagine you wouldn't take it all that personally, because you'd think that she was, well . . . mad.

So why would you get hurt when your 14-year-old daughter bursts into tears and screams 'Fuck you — I hate you!' just because you asked her why she hadn't cleaned up the bathroom? You see, it has always been my view that adolescence is more like a mental illness than a developmental phase. They are not right in the head, and the science would seem to be on my side with this one.

Now, I need to be very clear that I am in no way trivializing the genuine distress and heartbreak experienced by families with teenagers with genuine psychiatric illnesses. Far from it, because I've worked with many families struggling to deal with these very real issues.

What I *am* saying — and I'm saying this unreservedly — is that you shouldn't take your girl too seriously when she does mad stuff or says mad stuff. It's not all her fault. Some of it is, but some of it is simply an artefact of not being fully connected. Her grid still has some work needing doing. So if you think that when she says she hates you she really means it, then you're a mug. She doesn't. If she's still saying it in her mid-20s, that's a different story; but in those turbulent teenage years, it's usually a far more sensible course of action to simply put it down to the ranting of Mad Aunty Harriet.

The good news is that, with time and a little patience, Mad Aunty Harriet will make a complete recovery.

The only question that matters

As you can see, the brain stuff is all fairly interesting and does seem to hold a few clues as to why teenagers are so . . . well . . . teenager-like. They may look more and more like adults, but that doesn't mean they are — in fact, as we've seen in some areas of their functioning, quite the opposite is true. So the really big question is this: in the swirling hormonal, pubertal, neurobiological hurly-burly that defines the world of teenage girls, what can you do to make sure that you both get out alive and in one piece?

Luckily I do have some answers to that, but I'm going to need another chapter.

Tips on
Adolescence

☆ During adolescence, her brain will be undergoing some fairly major rewiring.

☆ It isn't a straight line: sometimes she'll seem quite mature, and sometimes she'll behave like a little girl.

☆ During this time, she will be less able to accurately evaluate things like risk, but will probably feel she is better than ever at doing it.

☆ Most of all: remember Mad Aunty Harriet.

16

How to survive your teenage daughter

So, down to the nitty-gritty: how *do* you survive your teenage daughter?

You just gotta hang in there

One evening after I'd just finished a parenting talk about teenagers, a man came up to me as I was packing up. He looked like a cop. I don't know what it is about cops, but you can almost always spot them. It turned out he was the local sergeant and, for his sins, he had two daughters. One was 11 and the other was 15. The little one was doing OK, but the older one was apparently driving him completely batshit.

'That Mad Aunty Harriet stuff is right', he said. 'My girl's gone completely loco. It's like she became this she-demon overnight. She used to be lovely when she was little, but now it's like she's a raving lunatic. All I have to do is open my mouth and she's off.'

'Sometimes they can be a little tricky,' I agreed.

'Seriously, I sometimes wonder if there really is something wrong with her. She doesn't seem to think like a normal person anymore. Sometimes she acts like she's 7, and sometimes she thinks she's 37. And if she doesn't get her way, or the wind blows funny, or it's that time of the month, or whatever the hell it is, she goes nuts.'

'So how do you handle it?' I asked him.

'To be honest, I just try and keep my head down most of the time. I mean, we've got rules and things about where she's allowed to go and what time she needs to be back, but apart from that I just try and leave her alone so I don't get her all riled up.'

'Understandable,' I said, 'but you gotta keep in mind all that stuff I was just talking about. Girls need their dads for all kinds of different reasons.'

He nodded. 'Yeah, I know, but ... you know ...'

'I know, but you really gotta hang in there.'

'It's funny,' he said, 'I think there's a much better chance my teenage daughter's gonna kill me through a stroke or something like that than any of the buggers I have to lock up at work.'

We laughed, both of us keenly aware that he was only half-joking.

The good news is that it's actually fairly easy to survive your teenage daughter — much easier than all the complicated biology of the previous two chapters might at first suggest. What's even better news still is that it's just as easy to be the kind of dad who gives her the best start to life she could possibly have. Sure, things are complicated, but that doesn't mean they actually have to *be* complicated.

It's actually a little bit like driving a car, in that you don't need to know all the technical details to make it work. Kids are a lot like that. All I've done is skim the surface of the physiology and neuroscience of adolescence: there's stuff in the science so technically complicated it's more acronyms than actual words. None of us need to understand it all to that level, though, because all that matters is how to drive the thing. I don't know what an alternator does, or even what it looks like, but I can back a trailer up the twistiest drive you can find. You don't need to know the nuts and bolts to get where you want to go, even if sometimes you're going backwards and the road is winding.

In that spirit, then, here are my suggestions for how to get the job done. There's no science behind any of this — it's only what I think. Nothing more, nothing less.

Don't run

Usually puberty is when most dads feel like backing quietly away to some shed somewhere and taking up cabinet-making. You might have had no previous interest in cabinet-making, but suddenly it might feel like the thing you most want to do in the whole world. If it were just the uncomfortable realization that your little girl is no longer little, that would be bad enough — but it's all the psychological stuff as well. It's the fact that dad jokes no longer work, that she seems frustrated and angry a lot of the time, and that sometimes she cries for no discernible reason, and sometimes makes absolutely no sense at all. She wants to be her own woman, and chart her own course, which wouldn't be so bad if she weren't 11.

Run, the little voice whispers somewhere deep inside. *Run to the shed, lock the door, and build cabinets for however long it takes until things return to normal.*

Like I said to my friendly police sergeant above, that's perfectly understandable, but, whatever you do, don't listen to that sensible-sounding little voice.

The weird thing is that, even though she might start acting like she needs you less and less, and that her world is more and more different from yours, she actually needs you now more than ever. She wants to be free, but she also needs to know that she isn't free. She needs to know that she's part of something more solid than bricks and steel; she needs to know that she's part of your life.

Always.

No matter how much she acts like she wants you to go away, don't be fooled. Your job is simply to ride the waxing and waning cycles of the teenage years with a calm determination.

Be there.

Sometimes be there loud, and sometimes be there quietly; just make sure that you're there.

Make sure she knows you're interested in her life

It's important to be interested in her life, but it's doubly important for her to *know* that you're interested. I am constantly amazed, and I have to say a little saddened, to hear so many adult women talk about how they didn't feel like their dads were interested in their lives when they were growing up. Lots of women talk about how their dads took them places and picked them up, but many of them say they weren't really sure he was interested in *them*.

Now, I'm a dad, and even though I have sons I think that almost all dads *are* interested in our kids' lives; I just think we're sometimes not very good at *showing* them we are.

Sadly, I think this is particularly true when it comes to dads and daughters, because their daughters can sometimes feel so foreign, and they seem so easily offended and upset, that a lot of dads adopt a 'say nothing, do no harm' approach. Sure, these guys *are* interested, but in a passive way, much as one might be interested in a landmine but not necessarily want to piss it off.

Don't be one of those. Make sure she knows that you are interested in the ups and downs of her life. Don't worry too much about how to do that without upsetting her, because it's almost inevitable that you will upset her. You've already lost, so relax and don't over-think it.

If you're stuck on how to do that, I'll give you the best opening question in the history of the world. The only trick is to not flip it around like a business card at a sales convention, but use it with the gravitas that such a question demands. Only ask it when you have the time to gather up all the weird and wonderful things it will bring your way.

Here it is: So, how was your day?

Show her you love her every day

With the onset of puberty usually comes the onset of awkwardness about physical affection. Like we talked about back in Chapter 4, it's inevitable, particularly in a world where every time you turn on the television there's some news story about sexual abuse, or some made-for-television movie about it. Remember how the very first dad I talked to about this book said that the whole 'physical affection thing' was the biggest issue for him? Should he still hug his daughters? When was she too old to sit on his knee, or snuggle up in bed with him?

In many ways the world has become a bit of a paranoid and sad place. We're so consumed with stories of sexual abuse and wrongdoing that sometimes it's easy to forget that some things are as true now as they ever were. Kids want to feel loved, they need it.

And what's most important for you to know is that kids know the difference between love and abuse. It's pretty hard to get those two things confused. In addition to working with kids and families, I've also spent the past 20 years working with sexual offenders and with the people they have abused as well, and let me tell you here and now that kids know the difference between a hug and something darker.

So when is she too old for hugs and kisses?

I've said it at the beginning of this book and I'll say it again now, just in case you skipped Chapter 4: never.

It's inevitable that there will be times during her teenage years where she may want a little more space. That could last for minutes or it could last for months. Either way, you just need to be sensitive to the cues you're getting and pitch the physical affection stuff at a level she can handle.

If she is in a pull-back space, then pull back. That doesn't mean that you have to pull away totally, though. There are still plenty of ways you can show her that you love her.

◊ Tell her.

◊ Put a note on her pillow or a favourite chair.

◊ Draw silly pictures and put those in her schoolbag.

◊ Sit by her on the couch and watch telly together.

◊ Use technology like Twitter and Facebook to send her little electronic hugs; also links to silly YouTube videos.

◊ Leave a can of sardines on her pillow. When she asks you why you did that, tell her that in some cultures fathers express their love for their daughters by leaving gifts of fish.

◊ Buy her a pony (although obviously this one is a bit extreme and you probably want to think the implications through quite carefully). If you don't have the space for a real pony, you could buy her a stuffed pony from a taxidermist, or a plastic one.

The big message here is that it's important for her to feel loved, and so you need to find as many interesting and fun ways to show her that as you have the time, energy, and inclination to do. You don't have to make it your full-time job, or get all crazy and obsessive about it, just make an effort is all I'm saying.

Be the rock

There's no question that some girls go a little loco during the teenage years. I remember once a mum was telling me about her own adolescence, and she said that she could recall moments when she would experience overpowering waves of what she described as 'completely unwarranted rage'. It wasn't that anybody had done anything in particular to her — she simply got angry for no particular reason and needed to dump that on the world.

This is a little hard to understand for many dads, because we're fairly logical creatures. The usual male response is that if you're angry about something, there must be a reason, and therefore there must be a way to fix it. After all, who would want to be angry for no particular reason? That doesn't make any kind of sense.

Unfortunately, in the emotional landscape of the teenage girl it doesn't necessarily need to make any kind of sense, at least not the kind of sense that makes sense to us. It doesn't even need to make sense to her, but even that kind-of makes sense to her.

In the face of all that, it can all get a little confusing for many dads. They make the fundamental error of trying to make sense of something that makes no conventional sense. This is why one of the most important things you need to understand is that you need to be the rock. It's important to make the distinction here that I am not talking about The Rock, better known as Dwayne Johnson, former WWF wrestler and star of *The Scorpion King*. Few of us can aspire to his muscle-bound physique, but you can be the rock in your daughter's life.

The defining characteristic of a rock is that it's generally pretty solid, and it can go the distance. In fact they do go the distance, with little complaint or comment. You don't see rocks out protesting about global warming or oil prices. It's been my observation that they don't give a shit about all the issues that we get wound up about. Rocks know who they are, what they're about, and most of all they know that all things pass with time. If you were to ask a rock how they manage to do that, I think it would say that it all boils down to three things:

◊ patience

◊ certainty

◊ a sense of humour.

Your daughter needs you to be like that. You don't need to understand her moods all the time, and you don't need to understand the causes and solutions of all the dramas which surround her, but you *do* need to have almost limitless patience, a measured certainty that most things usually work out in time, and most of all a sense of humour.

Get clear about your limits and stick to them

It is the job of every child to try to rule the world. It's not their fault, and it's not a bad thing, it's simply the way of the world. This very morning my own son, having just been told by his mother to finish at least half the crusts he'd left on his plate (what is it with children and crusts?), sneakily pushed some under his plate when his mother wasn't looking and then asked if he'd eaten enough. I saw all this, but didn't rat him out. In all honesty it's probably because I understand the urge: none of us want to eat our crusts.

The problem is that when your girl hits her teenage years, she's inevitably going to want more freedom than she's necessarily equipped to handle. Again, there's nothing wrong with her wanting all this freedom — that's natural — but there's a lot wrong with you giving it to her. What you need to watch out for, though, is how incredibly resourceful, and sometimes forceful, she can be in her pursuit of these freedoms. Some of the ways she may set about doing this can include the following tactics, or WMDs (Weapons of Mass Disruption).

◊ Wearing you down by going on and on and on and on and on and on and on and on and on.

◊ Threats of running away or some other equally drastic consequence if you say no.

◊ Saying that she hates you to get you to buckle and do what she wants so she'll like you again.

◊ Sulking.

◊ Playing you off against her mother.

◊ Trying to make you feel guilty.

◊ Wearing her pseudo-broken heart on her sleeve when you say she can't go somewhere.

◊ Ganging up on you with her friends.

◊ Asking for some huge thing she doesn't want (eg, going to a gang tattoo convention) and then 'settling' for what she really wanted (eg, going to her friend's place).

The way you deal with all of these is the same: you get clear about what your limits are, and you stick to them. I'm going to talk about how you do this in more depth in the next chapter, but just for now all you need to think about is getting very clear about your limits and sticking to them. As with all things, those limits will change as she gets older (and hopefully wiser), but at each stage you need to know where the line is drawn in the sand and stick to it.

Remember Mad Aunty Harriet

We talked about this in the previous chapter, but it's worth me saying again that you need to keep this one front and centre as you traverse the interesting teenage years. Your daughter might look more and more like an adult, but that doesn't mean that she is. Her brain is going through all kinds of changes, and so if you expect her to have the same skills of analysis and reasoning as an adult you will be sadly disappointed. Remember that she is likely to get more emotional now than she will be once everything has been successfully wired into the grid. Take it seriously — just don't take it too seriously.

Tips on

How to survive your teenage daughter

☆ Don't run.

☆ Make sure she knows that you're interested in her life.

☆ Show her you love her every day.

☆ Be the rock.

☆ Be clear about your limits and stick to them.

☆ Remember Mad Aunty Harriet.

17

Managing behaviour: Hell hath no fury like an angry teenage girl

There is no doubt that your biggest enemy during this time is fear. It's natural for dads to feel protective towards their kids, we all do, but I think fathers of daughters feel this particularly strongly. No matter how hard you try, it can be hard to completely shake the notion that she is some kind of fragile flower that needs closeting and protecting. It's hard to shake a lifetime of cultural conditioning overnight.

The proliferation of women in the armed forces and law enforcement throughout the world would seem to suggest that girls can hold their own, but dads sometimes struggle with that. By way of an interesting little example, I once watched a female cop demonstrate a technique she'd been shown about how you can kill someone with an envelope. I'm not sure when you would have the need for such a technique — presumably in some kind of hostile office-type situation — but it was a pretty clear example of how girls really can do anything.

Including killing people with envelopes.

Fear is the enemy here because it will push you out of the driver's seat. If you give in to fear, you will quickly become ineffectual, and she will have far more freedom than is good for her. Paradoxically, she is more likely to get into trouble if you let her use fear to push you around. This is typically how it starts.

Her: I'm going out tonight.

You: What?

Her: I'm going out tonight.

You: Where?

Her: Some friends.

You: Some friends? Who?

Her: You don't know them.

You: Well, where are you going?

Her: Some guys from school are having a party.

You: Which guys?

Her: You don't know them.

You: What are their names? Where do they live?

Her: I don't know where they live. Julie's picking me up on the way.

You: Well, you're not going unless I know who these boys are and where the party is.

Her: *Dad.*

You: No. I want to know who they are and where it is.

Her: I'm not going to ask Julie that — she'll think I'm a baby.

You: I don't care.

Her: *Dad. Don't be such an egg!*

You: I'm not being an egg, but I want to know.

Her: Well I'm *not* going to ask, and you can't stop me from going.

You: Yes, I can.

Her: How?

You: (Uncomfortable blank pause.)

Her: I'm going, and you can't stop me.

You: I want you back here by 11, then.

Her: *Dad, you can't be serious? Eleven? On a Friday night?*

You: OK, well midnight then, but no later.

Her: I'll try.

You: (somewhat weakly) Yeah, well you better, young lady.

Conversations like that one have been going on between dads and daughters since the Stone Age. They know that you're worried about them, so they use the whole 'If you don't let me, I'll go anyway' routine. They bank on the fact that we'll be so desperate to have them home we'll settle for their rules, given that the only options they put on the table are their rules or no rules.

Except that's not even what she wants.

What she really wants

Imagine a world with no rules — and no, I'm not talking about the cool zombie post-apocalyptic world we all dream of, but the everyday world with no rules. What a zoo it would be. As much as we all struggle with the various rules we must adhere to in life, by and large rules do make the world a better place, or at least they make it a little easier to deal with.

Sure there are stupid rules — like in the city I live in, where the town-planning people seem to have embarked on an ambitious and completely insane plan to ban any right turns anywhere in the city — but mostly the rules make the life a lot more liveable. If there were no rules, or we could simply pick and choose the ones we wanted to obey, it would get tricky pretty quickly. The simple act of crossing the road would suddenly become an act fraught with the opportunity for random and unpredictable death. Buying a coffee would no longer be straightforward, but could instead become intensely frustrating and rife with injustice.

'I'm not serving you,' the person behind the counter might say.

'Why not?' you ask.

'Because you're funny-lookin'. I don't like funny-lookin' people, so I'm not serving you.'

'What the—'

'Get out, monkey boy. Get out of my café, you weird-appearing person.'

We complain about the rules and regulations a lot, but without them our lives would be a lot worse than they are with them. Civilization depends on rules. Without them, funny-looking people can't buy coffee and anarchy follows shortly thereafter.

This is something you need to keep in mind when your daughter is railing against the rules. She might act like she hates them, and she might really hate them, but she'd hate it a lot more without them. Rules may stop her from doing stuff she might feel like doing, but they also give her a reason not to do things she doesn't want to do. More importantly, rules also give her a reason not to do things she feels like doing but also knows she shouldn't do.

Basically, rules are good, so don't be bullied or badgered into abandoning them. One of the most important things you can do for her is to make sure you have some good, sound, agreed-upon rules in your home. She might not thank you for it now, but she will later.

Family rules

The trick with family rules is to have a few simple ones — and stick to them. If you have to write them down to remember them all, then you've got too many. As soon as you start having to write stuff down, you're into the territory that lawyers occupy and that's probably a little over-the-top for most of us.

My suggestion would be that somewhere between three to five rules is best. You can also have some general rules for life at home, like the following.

◇ Treat people with respect.

◇ Do agreed-upon jobs within agreed-upon timeframes.

◇ Respect each other's personal space and possessions.

But you can also have a set of rules for going out as well.

◇ Be where you say you will be.

◇ Be home at the agreed time.

◇ If the plan changes, ring home first to see if that is OK.

Nice and simple is the trick. The more complicated they are, the more they're open to interpretation. If you have clauses and subclauses, all you're doing is opening up avenues for debate. The thing here is that you need to operate on the basis of *ad iudicium*, which is a fancy Latin way of saying common sense. You should make this the underpinnings of the criminal justice system in your home. Have as few rules as possible, and then use *ad iudicium* as the guiding principle for how those rules are interpreted and enacted.

The other crucial component of family rules with teenagers is that the rules need to be negotiated. If you simply impose a bunch of rules without any discussion, then they're far more likely to want to go right out and break them. Some parents worry about the idea of negotiating rules with their kids. They worry that if you let the peasants in on the law-making they'll come up with a whole bunch of wacky and completely unreasonable laws, but the truth is they don't. Most kids think that the rules their parents put in place are fairly reasonable. Most 14-year-old girls know that it is both unreasonable and unrealistic to have a rule that they should be able to stay out as late as they want.

Quite aside from anything else, you will need to constantly adjust the rules as she grows older anyway. A rule that is utterly reasonable for a 12-year-old girl might be completely insane for a 17-year-old girl. The goalposts will continue to shift, so you need to make sure that the family rules account for this.

'What're ya gonna do about it?'

At some point, she's going to ask that question. She'll either do it out loud, or she'll ask it in her head — either way, she's going to ask it. All kids do. This question marks an important transition in their lives, and the beginning of what is usually one of the messiest parts of the family life cycle. It's messy, because at this point it can be a little confusing trying to work out who's in charge. For a while, no one will be in charge, not really. Oh sure, there will be protestations and deputations, from both sides usually, but there's no way around the fact that at some point the amount of control you have will seriously decline, and she still won't be quite ready to assume full and competent charge.

If you're heading into her teenage years and you think you can actually control any of the following, then you are operating under a serious level of denial:

◇ studying

◇ smoking cigarettes

◇ alcohol and drug use

◇ who she is friends with

◇ whether or not she has sex

◇ who her boyfriend is

◇ or who her girlfriend is, for that matter

◇ the music she listens to

◇ what she wears

◇ where she goes.

You can influence all of those things — some more than others, obviously — but you can't *control* any of them. The time when you could control her is long gone. The word you should focus on now is *influence*, because that's the only option you have left. Usually this is the biggest issue that parents struggle with, and usually where things can go catastrophically wrong if they're going to. If you're aiming for control, you will almost certainly fail. If you do somehow manage to control her, you will be doing her no favours: she doesn't need to be controlled, she needs to be influenced.

This doesn't mean you are automatically relegated to playing a passive role in her life, because that would be a mistake, too. She needs you to be actively involved in helping her to manage her life; just don't make the mistake of thinking you can control her.

You can't.

Don't be her friend

This is hugely important, because you must not be her friend. She only has one dad, and whilst she can always make new friends, she can't make a new dad. This is sometimes more of a challenge for mums in my experience. Some mums make the colossal mistake of thinking that if they build a relationship with their daughter that is more akin to a friendship, then their daughters will be more likely to talk to them about what's going on in their lives.

Yeah, right.

If you try to make your kid your friend, you deprive her of the most important resource she has in the world: a parent. Friends generally go along with what you're thinking, whereas parents step in and make the hard calls. Parents tell you off when you need it. Friends just giggle.

Besides, you'll never be her friend anyway. A parent who tries to be their kid's friend is like the nerdiest kid in school trying to be friends with the coolest kids in school. They'll use you for whatever they can get and then make fun of you behind your back.

It can feel like you're doing the right thing by trying to make her your friend, because it will feel like you're 'close'. You might even avoid a lot of direct conflict, which will also give the completely false impression that things are going well. In my humble opinion, though, it will always be a false impression, because the reality is that she will be friends with her friends, and she'll just be some other weird thing with you.

You're not her friend. You're her dad.

Yeah, yeah . . . but what do I actually do?

Fair enough question. Enough with all these general background, context-setting non-specifics — let's get down to the brass tacks of how to actually do the sharp end of parenting stuff. Whilst it's true that you can't control her, you can be a pretty powerful influence in her life. The way you do that is by building a set of expectations around her that she gets rewarded for if she meets them, and has to pay for is she doesn't. This is how the world works for all of us, so it's what you should do for her, too. The government can't control us, but they can do a bunch of things to make us think pretty carefully about our options and how we'd like to conduct ourselves.

All you do is set up the context; she makes her own decisions about what she does. That's a subtle but incredibly important distinction. You can't control her, but you do control large parts of the context she exists in.

Here it is in three simple steps.

1 *Get clear about your limits and stick to them*
   I talked about this in the previous chapter, and it's fundamentally important to get your head around this one. She wants limits, even if she doesn't, so give them to her. This is where the family rules come in. Remember these rules need to be simple, have a basis in common sense, and be negotiated and agreed to by all.

2 *Follow through*
   The day you don't follow through with some promised consequence is the day that anarchy starts moving into the corner office. If you say something will happen, make sure it does.

3 *Do the previous two steps over and over until the message gets through*
   All you really need is those first two, but two steps just looks funny, so I've added in this cunning little third step.

I mean it, though: just keep doing the first two over and over until she gets whatever message you need her to get.

Of course the big issue most parents struggle with is what to do if she calls your bluff. How do you punish her?

It's become a rather unfashionable word, 'punishment', but that doesn't mean we still can't use it. In fact, if anything we should try to use more of the things that have fallen out of modern favour when it comes to raising kids, because a lot of it's just plain silly. (As a for instance, it's now frowned upon to use children as powder monkeys in naval boats, because people say it isn't safe for kids to handle gunpowder and cannon balls. Surely it's better to get the little ones to fetch the cannon balls, because adults are more likely to hurt their backs?) The specific issue that the modern world has with 'punishment' is that now it's supposed to be about being nice all the time. In the modern world, it's all about rewarding good behaviour and 'helping them to reflect on their poor choices' when they're bad.

Not for me, it isn't. I've spent a lot of years working with really difficult kids, and it's long been my experience that it's all about getting the balance right between the carrot and the stick. (See, just using that metaphor will have some people recoiling in horror. It's just a metaphor, anxious types, calm down.)

What I mean is that you need to give your children reasons to be good (incentives and rewards), but you also need to give them reasons not to be bad (punishment). That's just plain old common sense, and it's also how the world works. Although you could actually make a fairly convincing argument that none of us are rewarded for our good behaviour, we just get punished for our bad behaviour. What happens if you're caught speeding? Or if you don't pay your taxes? Or if you dump a truckload of horseshit at some politician's door? They don't talk to us about our poor choices: we either get fined, or if it's really bad we go to jail.

Being punitive doesn't work, but punishment does. Being

punitive is effectively just being mean and controlling. That is always going to end badly. Punishment, on the other hand, is simply helping them to link up action with reaction. If you do something you know you're not supposed to do, then most times no good will come of it. I want my kids to learn that no good can come from doing things they know they're not allowed to do.

Obviously there are times when you are going to want them to break the rules, particularly if those rules are oppressive or unjust, but the rules you make for them hopefully won't involve any great moral or social injustices, in which case it is probably going to be in their best interests to follow them.

So how do you do that?

Read on.

The Ladder of Certain Doom

If you've read any of my other books you will already have come across this, so feel free to skip this bit if you've seen it before. If you haven't, then this section is well worth a read, because this is my very own little behaviour management tool, developed years ago in a fit of inspired deviousness. It's now been tried and tested in homes around the world, and most people find that if used as directed it can fix most behavioural ills.

The reason I say 'most' is that some people hate it. Most of these people are little people, and the reason they hate it is because it works. Perhaps as testament to the effectiveness of the technique, a couple of years ago I received a hate poem from a 10-year-old girl. Her parents had started using the ladder and she hated it, and she wanted to share her thoughts with me in verse.

I must be doing something right if I'm getting hate poems from 10-year-old girls.

The only real prerequisite is that the kids have to be old enough to understand the concept of time, particularly decreasing time. They need to be able to get the fact that, when you take time off them, that means they will be going to bed earlier. For older girls you can substitute going to bed early with some other variable (eg, curfew time, computer time, pocket money, telephone time).

Here's how it works.

1 Draw up a simple Ladder on a piece of paper as shown to the right. The Ladder starts at your daughter's normal bedtime and then goes down in half-hour steps until the time she gets home from school. With younger girls, you can make the steps 10 or 15 minutes.

| 8.00pm |
| 7.30pm |
| 7.00pm |
| 6.30pm |
| 6.00pm |
| 5.30pm |
| 5.00pm |
| 4.30pm |
| 4.00pm |
| 3.30pm |

2 Put the Ladder up on the fridge where she can see it.

3 Place a fridge magnet at the very top of the chart. The magnet now becomes the 'flag' that tells her what time she's going to bed. Each child gets their own distinctive magnet or 'flag'.

4 Every day starts with the flag at the top of the Ladder, 8.00pm in this example.

5 If there is bad behaviour, then the flag moves down a rung. If the bad behaviour doesn't stop in a given period of time (usually a 1-2-3 count), then the flag moves down another a rung.

6 Similarly, if you ask her to do a task within a set period of time (best measured with the microwave timer) and it isn't done, the flag moves down a rung.

7 The flag keeps moving down until your request is complied with, or the flag reaches the current time and then she goes to bed. If the flag gets to 3.30pm and it is 3.30pm, then off to bed she goes.

8 **This next bit is very important:** If she has *lost* time off

her bedtime, she can *earn* her way back ***up*** the rungs by doing a *payback job* (see below).

9 Really good days, where she hasn't lost any time, are rewarded with special treats, as are really good weeks. You should decide what is a realistic number of good days to qualify for a weekly reward for your girl. (It should be a bit of a stretch, but definitely achievable. You might start with two good days and gradually increase this as her behaviour improves.) In this way, the Ladder also doubles as a sticker chart.

Payback jobs

Payback jobs are fundamentally important to how the Ladder works, because payback jobs are the vehicle for getting out of negative cycles and back into positive ones. The purpose of the payback job is to encourage her to enter into positive behaviour. Some examples of payback jobs are given below:

◊ sweeping the drive

◊ emptying the dishwasher

◊ hanging out the washing

◊ tidying up her room

◊ vacuuming

◊ cleaning the toilet

◊ washing the car.

It is important that she chooses which payback job she does, because choice increases the chance of compliance. I suggest that parents have a small box of cards that children can choose from, each with a separate payback job on it and the steps that each job entails. An example is shown at the top of the next page.

By establishing the exact components of the job, you avoid a debate about whether or not the job is finished. The card acts

> **Emptying the dishwasher**
> 1. Carefully take each piece out of the dishwasher.
> 2. Make sure it is dry.
> 3. Put it away in the right place.
> 4. Close the dishwasher.
> 5. Wipe away any water on the bench.

as an objective checklist: all you have to do is look at the card, look at what she's done, and then the answer is clear. If there is still water on the bench, you simply say: 'That's good, but you've forgotten Step 5. Tell me when it's done, and I'll let you move the flag up.'

The size of the job should be reflected in the size of the payback. So, for example, she might get to go up two rungs (one hour) for cleaning her room, and only one rung (half an hour) for sweeping the drive. This will depend on her age as well. When she completes the payback job, make sure you toss a bit of praise around so she feels good for making the decision to become a reasonable human being again.

How do you use the Ladder with older girls?

Once you have the concept of decreasing time with non-compliance and increasing time when they pay it back by doing some job or other, it becomes easier to see how you can use this with older girls. There will come a time when it's getting a little silly to send them to bed early (usually from 13 or 14 onwards), so you need to substitute early bedtime for some other thing. Some options for things you can use are listed below:

◇ curfew time

◇ time on the computer

◇ time on the phone

◇ pocket money/allowance
◇ clothes (progressively take them away so she doesn't have many fashion options)
◇ distance you are prepared to drive her in the car to her friends' places.

This is just a start. I'm sure that if you set your mind to it there will be all kinds of other ways you can think of to apply the Ladder of Certain Doom.

Why does it work?

I think the Ladder works for a number of reasons. It's quite a complicated little tool, but it has a very clear and easy-to-understand structure. What's more, it puts all the responsibility on them, rather than on you. You don't have to calm her down if she's yelling and screaming; she does. All you need to do is move the flag down until she quietens down. This is important, because it teaches them that they are in control of their emotions and not the other way around.

It's all about balance

The trick with teenage girls is that it's all about balance. You don't want to give her too much freedom. She might say that she wants that, but she doesn't, and in any case it's not good for her. Having said that, you don't want to be such a control freak that she doesn't have any freedom. If you're running every aspect of her life and telling her what to do every second of the day, you will end up hurting her.

Girls need space just as boys do. No one wants every aspect of their lives controlled and managed, and none of us wants anarchy. Some reasoned, sensible, negotiated middle ground is where you need to be.

It's also the best place for her to be.

Putting it all together: Kara
(the girl from the preface, remember?)

After Kara's melodramatic stampede from my office that day, I talked a while further with her mum and dad about how to manage things a little differently. Sadly for them, fixing Kara isn't possible — although happily this was mainly because she wasn't broken. In fact she was doing exactly what a 13-year-old girl should be doing, albeit in a slightly rude and offensive manner. Even then, her rudeness wasn't excessive. Not all teenagers are terrible, but most of them are a bit like Kara: they have their moments, but are largely bearable. In her case, there were a few simple things I suggested her parents do which might help things along.

◊ First, they needed to get their heads around her changing head. Rather than freaking out and thinking their daughter really was exhibiting the early warning signs of a female axe-murderer, they needed to understand the 'Mad Aunty Harriet' metaphor, and the brain development stuff which underlies it. In my experience, once you've got that squarely under your belt it makes some of the slightly unhinged moments of adolescence seem a little more understandable.

◊ Next, they needed to get some simple rules in place, and in particular some rules about how everyone talked to each other.

◊ Then, they needed to apply some consequences (although actually I mean punishments) if she broke those rules. They decided to use the LoCD and apply decreasing time on the computer, which provided them with plenty of leverage because she was addicted to Bebo.

◊ On the swing side of that, the more reasonable she was, and the more respectful she was when she talked to them, the more they were open to negotiating increased time.

◊ Peter also made a promise to try to spend a little bit more time with her, rather than simply backing away and leaving her alone for fear of upsetting her.

I called them a couple of weeks later and, even though things weren't perfect (and trust me, they never are), the situation had calmed down a lot. Both

Peter and Amanda were worrying less about Kara being 'out of control' and were letting her simply make her own decisions about whether or not she was going to stick to the rules. As is always the case, once they relaxed a bit, and got a clearer structure, things started to settle.

'We've actually had a fairly pleasant run for the past week or so,' Peter told me.

'Miracles can happen,' I said.

Although, to be honest, this kind of stuff is less about miracles and more about getting the everyday physics straight.

Action and reaction is all you need to keep in mind.

Tips on
Managing behaviour

☆ Despite what she says, or how she acts, she wants rules, and boundaries, and structure.

☆ Family rules are important. Keep them brief and clear.

☆ Don't be her friend, be her parent.

☆ Use tools like the Ladder of Certain Doom.

☆ It's all about balance: not too tight, not too loose.

18

The semi-myth of the gentler sex

I've never bought all that stuff about women being the gentler sex. If you listen to the sisterhood talk, you'd think that if women ran the world it would be a kinder, gentler place, where trains ran on time, war was no more, and everyone would feel loved and content.

Bollocks.

Margaret Thatcher did run quite a chunk of the world for 11 years, and in that time she started a war of her own over the Falklands Islands — a barren, windswept series of islands just off the coast of Argentina — and presided over one of the most ruthless experiments in economic and social change of the 20th century. Actually, there were lots of people in Britain who thought Margaret Thatcher was ruthless in all kinds of ways, and, among all the words I've heard used to describe her, 'gentle' was not one of them.

It wasn't only her, though. For example, if you're ever hijacked you should pray that your hijackers are men, because if they decide to kill the hostages they'll just blow up the plane. Women hijackers tend to bring whole boxes of stuff to make your ending all that more unpleasant.

The reason I don't buy that whole gentler sex routine is that I really do think women are equal to men in every way — including that if women had been in charge of the world for as long as men have been, I think they would have stuffed it up equally badly. Maybe there'd be one or two slight differences (like, for instance, having more women's toilets in public places so they wouldn't have to queue), but by and large I think we'd still be living in a world facing all kinds of conflicts, a global climate crisis, and various other hoo-hahs and to-dos. I don't think it would all be poetry and harmony.

But surely it's true that men are more violent than women?
Kind of.
What do you mean 'kind of'?
Just what I said: kind of.
Explain.
OK, but I'll need a subheading to do it.
Help yourself.

Uncomfortable science

Not all science is comfortable; in fact, some science makes us decidedly uneasy. I'd imagine there was a fairly uncomfortable silence when Galileo first stood up and said to the Pope that, actually, we revolve around the sun, not the other way around. This went down like a cup of cold sick with Pope Urban VII who, even though he sounds like a right hip dude, wasn't. Galileo said it again in a book, even after the Pope warned him to back off, and then he said it yet again to the Roman inquisition during a Papal trial, which, not surprisingly, didn't go so well for him. He was found guilty of heresy and put under house arrest in 1634. He went completely blind in 1638 and suffered from insomnia and a painful hernia. He finally died in 1642. Who can blame him?

Obviously I'm hoping that what I'm about to say next doesn't go quite so badly for me. I'm clearly not wanting to end up locked in my house, blind, with a painful hernia, and not able to sleep, but sometimes things have to be said, even if they do make us a bit uncomfortable.

You see, I grew up as a shrink through the 1990s, which was a time of dreadfully dour political correctness. During those years, men were bad, and women were good, and that was about as far as the analysis went. Men were offenders/perpetrators, and women were victims. To say anything else was tantamount to heresy. I went to many a conference where men were admonished to 'take responsibility for their violence' and were told that we should do this under the watchful eye of the sisterhood, who would ensure that we didn't creep off and start colluding with all those violent men, as it was almost certainly in our natures to do. It wasn't only the women saying this either; most of it was said by the men themselves. The whole thing was a bit sackcloth and ashes.

So I grew up believing that we really were the bad guys, and that violence was a male problem. Imagine my surprise when I later discovered that it wasn't. How do we know this? Well, remember our old friends from the Dunedin Multidisciplinary Health and Development Research Unit at Otago University? Remember their study which has been running for 37 years now and has been following up that same group all that time?

In 1997, some of the researchers working on the data that had been collected so far published a scientific paper looking at gender differences in partner violence. What they found was about as close to social heresy as you can get (see table next page).

This was a bit of a doozy, yet somehow the politics of 'family violence' has pretty much ignored the issue of female violence. They just sort-of stepped around it, mumbling something about how these figures cloud the issue that most female violence is committed by way of self-defence, and that male violence is far more serious because more women are hurt by men. Curiously, the argument seems to be that we shouldn't worry too much about female violence because it's inconsequential. In the 1990s, if I'd said that some male violence was 'inconsequential' I would

Rates of Partner Violence Committed by Women and Men

	Women (%)	Men (%)
Verbal aggression	94.6	85.8
Minor physical violence	35.8	21.8
Severe physical violence	18.6	5.7
Any physical violence	37.2	21.8

Source: L Magdol *et al* (1997). Gender differences in partner violence in a birth cohort of 21-year-olds: bridging the gap between clinical and epidemiological approaches. *Journal of Consulting and Clinical Psychology* 65(1), 68–78.

have been hung, drawn and quartered. They would have said I was colluding by saying things like that, and they'd have been right.

The problem with scientists, though, is that they're a pesky bunch, and the good ones tend not to let little things like gender politics get in the way of the facts. So it was that 11 years later David Fergusson and his colleagues from the Christchurch Health and Development Study (CHDS) published a further paper looking at the issue of men's and women's violence in intimate relationships. The CHDS was begun in 1977, and has followed 1,265 children born during a four-month period that year, initially following them up yearly, and then at slightly longer intervals. And what did they find?

◊ Violence occurred in 70% of relationships.

◊ Men and women reported similar levels of perpetration and victimization.

◊ The spectrum of violent behaviours committed by men and women was similar.

◊ Both men and women engaged in serious acts of physical violence.

Clearly what these studies are telling us is that violence is not just a 'male issue' — it's an 'everybody issue'. Both men and women perpetrate violence in intimate relationships, and so we need to address these issues with our sons *and* our daughters. Interestingly, the CHDS also produced some pretty good evidence of the factors which might predict children being violent in later life:

◊ a family background of multiple social, economic, and related deprivations

◊ having parents who themselves came from a disadvantaged background

◊ poor health care as a baby

◊ multiple changes of parents

◊ crap parenting practices

◊ for girls in particular, problem behaviours in childhood were a stronger predictor of later violence than for boys.

A list like that is very encouraging for fathers bringing up girls, because, apart from your background, every single one of them you can do something about. We can't change where we come from, but we don't have to let that define how we raise our girls. So apart from that one, they are *all* things that are in your control.

Which I think is bloody good news.

Are girls becoming more violent?

It's hard not to get the impression that girls are becoming more violent, because most weeks you will see media reports that are telling us they are. I'd also have to say that, as someone who has spent the better part of the past two decades working on the frontlines of youth offending, it certainly *feels* like they are. If you look at trends in arrest rates for girls, you will also see that there have been substantial increases in the number of females arrested for violent offences over the past couple of decades.

There are all kinds of possible reasons for this, and it's the kind of thing that academics and researchers will probably spend the next who-knows-how-long trying to figure out.

In my view, the reason we're seeing this increased rate of female offending probably reflects a combination of factors, including the fact we're now really only starting to acknowledge that girls can be violent, and that it can be serious. If we look, we're far more likely to find. Female violence has likely always been there, it's just now we're starting to take note of it, and to come in with a more 'law and order' based response to it. An almost inevitable consequence of that is a bit of a moral panic over the issue of female violence. For a long time, girls were pretty much absent from the debate on delinquency; now that we've decided to include them, there's a danger of girls becoming the 'flavour of the day', as these things are often wont to do. The trick with all these 'social issues' is to keep them in balance, to keep our feet on the ground, and to deal with what is actually in front of us rather than some hyped-up version of some new plague of girl violence.

Sure, some girls are violent, as are some boys, but many of them are quite nice. In my experience all kids start life being 'quite nice', but life sometimes has a way of messing with this. Our job as dads is to do the best we can to make sure she learns it's better to be nice than nasty.

'Inconsequential violence'

Many, many years ago in a past life I was a volunteer ambulance officer. I was student at the time, and for a period during my undergraduate degree I was the 'second guy' on one of the crews that worked the nightshift. Basically, there was a trained paramedic and a volunteer on each crew. We volunteers usually passed stuff and helped carry the stretcher, although when things got really messy there was a lot more scope for getting in there and getting your latex gloves dirty.

One night we got called out to a house at some time around 3.00am. I can't remember the exact time, but I know it was in the wee small hours when it feels like the world has somehow disappeared and left a weird empty shell of itself behind. The initial information said that a man had sustained a head injury and was bleeding profusely. As it turned out, he had. We found him slumped in the living room of the small flat, with a blood-soaked tea towel pressed up against his head. He was dressed, and had obviously been up for hours, as had his partner who hovered about looking both concerned but also very bloody angry. They were both in their late teens/early 20s.

'What happened, mate?' my crew chief asked, as he set about peeling back the bloody towel to try to inspect the wound.

'We just had a bit of an argument,' he said, 'and it got a bit out of hand.'

'It certainly looks that way. What happened to your head?'

'I threw a plate and it hit him by accident,' she chimed in from behind.

She sure looked like a plate-thrower to me, especially at 3.00am.

'It's no big deal,' the guy said. 'It just got a bit out of hand. It was just a stupid accident.'

'You want to be more careful, next time,' said my boss, as he looked up at the young woman. 'You could have seriously hurt this guy.'

'Yeah, well he shouldn't have *fucking* been going on about how much he hates my old boyfriend and it *wouldn't* have happened.'

I was surprised how quickly she sparked up, and I felt my own pulse raise a little, comforted only by the fact that there were no plates within arm's reach.

'It's alright,' said my boss in a practised tone that was both soothing and authoritative. 'We'll just get him into the ED and let them have a look at it.'

She came in with us, and she bickered with him the whole way in. The last time I saw them, she was sitting beside his bed in the ED as the house surgeon looked at the wound. She still had an angry, surly, mean look on her face, and I remember thinking I was bloody glad I wasn't going home to someone like that. I also remember that nothing happened to her. There was no police notification, no statements, no nothing.

They simply stitched up his head and he went home.

Just an argument between a guy and his girlfriend that got a little out of hand. If she'd been the one bleeding I'm sure he would have been reported, even way back then. But she wasn't the victim.

He was.

Inconsequential violence.

Moral of the story

So what fathers of daughters would be wise to take from all this is that we need to educate our daughters about how to have respectful relationships with people, just as we do our boys. It isn't only teaching them that no one has the right to hurt them or intimidate them — it's also about teaching them that they don't have the right to do that to other people as well.

Tips on
The semi-myth of the gentler sex

☆ Research shows that males are generally more violent than females *except* in relationships, where females are just as violent as men.

☆ This is not 'self-defence' or inconsequential violence, but serious and significant violence.

☆ As well as teaching your girl that she should never tolerate intimidation or violence, she also needs to understand she should not perpetrate it either.

19

Body image and eating disorders: the stranger in the mirror

One of the things you can't escape when you have girls is the whole issue of attractiveness, weight, and food. For many women, not just girls, these three issues are a constant backdrop to their lives. They worry about how they look, and about what they're eating a large percentage of the time. I think it's possible that there might be some women who are quite comfortable with how they look, but I'm not sure where they are. Many women worry that their tummy's fat, their bum is too big, their thighs are fat, and/or infinite combinations of all those things. Women, as a general rule, don't like their bodies.

The stuff which feeds this is out there in every glossy magazine, every TV show, every billboard, every comment. Like some nasty whispering hiss telling them over and over that thin is beautiful, thin is happy, thin is all that matters.

The extreme end of that continuum is where we find the eating disorders. Whilst boys can develop eating disorders as well, the problem is much greater in girls. It's all pretty scary stuff up this end of the line, because the impact of eating disorders on the developing body can be severe. There's some good news here, though, because after nearly four decades of research there are some pretty good indicators of how we can help our kids to resist the all-pervasive pull of these disorders, and especially the key role that fathers can play with their daughters.

It's also important for you to know that the early teen years (approximately 11–14 years of age) seem to be a time of heightened risk for girls. So this is an important time to be thinking very hard about the kinds of messages your daughter is exposed to, and, as we'll see later on in this chapter, a key time for you to ensure that her home is as supportive as possible.

Types of eating disorders

Before we get to that, though, I want to start by covering off the most common types of eating disorders: anorexia nervosa, bulimia nervosa, compulsive eating disorders, and EDNOS.

Anorexia nervosa

The core feature of anorexia nervosa is that the person severely restricts what they eat. This seems to be driven by both an intense fear of being fat, and a distorted view of their body. Girls suffering from anorexia don't just hate particular parts of their body — they hate all of it.

The following are signs and symptoms of anorexia nervosa, although bear in mind that not all girls experience all symptoms:

◊ avoiding meals

◊ dieting constantly

◊ having an extreme fear of putting on weight

◊ thinking they are fat when really they are too skinny

◊ not wanting to eat with the rest of the family

◊ severely reducing the amount and types of food they eat

◊ lying about what they have eaten

◊ becoming extremely deceptive about the amounts and types of foods they have eaten

◊ becoming very anxious or restless/guilty both during and immediately after eating

◊ developing weird food habits, such as preferences for particular colours or textures of food, or eating with 'special cutlery' like a teaspoon

◊ cutting food up into tiny pieces or arranging food in ritualistic ways

◊ developing rigid patterns around eating, such as eating only at certain times or only certain types of foods.

◊ saying they aren't hungry when they are

◊ focusing on weight constantly

◊ withdrawing socially and becoming uninterested in social and academic activities

◊ wearing baggy clothing

◊ exercising excessively

◊ losing a significant amount of weight

◊ having dry, pale skin

◊ stopping menstruating or having irregular periods.

Girls suffering from anorexia nervosa have a grossly distorted body image. They are very concerned about how they look and constantly wish they were thinner. They weigh themselves obsessively. They can be moody, argumentative, and extremely sensitive to criticism. Generally, these girls present as being very rigid and inflexible in their thinking and exhibit perfectionist tendencies. They will feel guilty about eating, have a low self-esteem, and may also suffer from depression and low moods.

Bulimia nervosa

The core feature of bulimia nervosa is that the person periodically binges on food in a way that feels quite out of control, and then compensates by vomiting, starving herself, exercising excessively, or sometimes by using laxatives excessively. People suffering from bulimia nervosa can seem outwardly quite confident and self-assured, but this is simply a façade to cover an internal world that is driven by insecurity and feelings of loss of control.

The following are signs and symptoms of bulimia nervosa, although again remember that a person might not necessarily display all of these symptoms:

◊ avoiding meals and not wanting to eat with the family
◊ appear increasingly restless after they eat, as their anxiety and guilt grows
◊ making excuses to go to the bathroom immediately following a meal (eg, to have a shower) and then inducing vomiting
◊ binging (large quantities of food are going missing, or you find food wrappers hidden in their room)
◊ spending all of their own money on food, or taking money to pay for food
◊ being constantly dissatisfied with their weight, with how they look, and being constantly focused on diets and dieting
◊ staying up late, or getting up in the middle of the night, so they can binge without being seen
◊ exercising excessively
◊ being low, apathetic, and having a depressed outlook on life
◊ withdrawing from social and academic activities
◊ having low self-esteem and being over-sensitive to criticism.

With bulimia nervosa, there can also be some quite distinct physical symptoms which result from constant binging and purging:

◊ pain and swelling in the abdomen
◊ swelling of the hands and feet

◊ swelling around the face and jawline

◊ feeling tired, sick, breathless and/or dizzy

◊ dental problems from eating sugary foods and constant vomiting

◊ intestinal bleeding, also from the constant vomiting.

The big issue with bulimia nervosa is not that people lose an amount of excessive weight, it's all the secondary health effects which flow on from the cycle of binging and purging. Stuffing yourself with food and then vomiting it all up again is really bad for your body.

Compulsive eating

The core feature of compulsive eating is essentially eating large amounts of food when you're not hungry. This might be in a binge, or it could be in continuous snacking throughout the day. This isn't as rare as you'd think either, because some studies have shown that as many as one in five teenagers have experienced a loss of control around eating. The following are signs and symptoms of compulsive eating, but again not everybody has all of them:

◊ binge eating

◊ eating until they are uncomfortably full

◊ eating much faster than usual

◊ eating alone because they are embarrassed about how much they are eating

◊ eating large amounts of food even when they aren't hungry

◊ feeling great amounts of disgust and shame both during and after over-eating

◊ gaining excessive weight.

The underlying experience of many people who suffer from

compulsive eating disorders is that eating is used as a way to manage difficult feelings like sadness, anger, fear, anxiety, or depression. The person can gain a brief respite from those feelings when they eat, but it's only very temporary and usually they come back with a renewed vengeance in a very short time.

Eating disorders not otherwise specified (EDNOS)

Whilst there has been a steady increase in the rate of eating disorders over the past several decades, a decrease in the level of severity of the symptoms has also been an observed. This has led to the development of a further category of eating disorders: Eating Disorders Not Otherwise Specified (EDNOS). This is now the most common eating disorder diagnosis amongst young people, and, despite the fact that people with EDNOS don't exhibit all the signs and symptoms necessary for a diagnosis of the other eating disorders, they can have as many difficulties. Just because girls don't always have all the symptoms doesn't mean they don't have all the problems.

What causes eating disorders?

That's a complicated one. As with many things in life, it seems there's no one single or simple explanation. Research from the past 40 years does seem to paint a fairly convincing picture that there are some pretty major players which can have an impact on the development of eating disorders. The good news here is that you can also have an impact on most of those areas as well. Effectively, it seems that it's a combination and interaction between family patterns of interaction, personal factors, media/ social influence, and dieting behaviour.

Not much of a surprise there, really. If you think about it, it's all pretty obvious that it's going to be a combination of how her family operates, how she sees herself, how the world impacts on her, and her relationship with food that's going to determine how much of an issue eating disorders are in her life.

The good news in amongst all this frightening information is that there are also some very clear suggestions for how you can effectively build your family so that your kids are best protected from having to deal with eating disorders. As with many of the issues our daughters face, the best people to help them deal with them are us.

The angry dad who wasn't angry even though he was

Carly was 15, and she looked terrible. I'm no doctor, but she was clearly very underweight for her age and looked both pale and sickly. I don't work with full-blown eating disorders as a general rule. The reason for this is that it's usually long-term work, and it's the kind of thing that's best done by multidisciplinary teams in specialist units. Having said that, I will work with families if they're in a 'holding pattern' on a waiting list for a specialist unit, but even then only if there is medical backup.

Carly was clearly in trouble, and I knew from the referral notes that she had been for some time. Her first admission to an eating disorders unit was when she was 13, and she was currently on a waiting list for what would be her third admission. According to her doctor, she wasn't on the dire end of the continuum just yet, but she was so close it was frightening.

She lived with her dad, and he had, by his own admission, always struggled to cope with her eating difficulties. Actually, it seemed to me that he'd struggled to cope with most things in his life, and his daughter was just one more thing on the list.

'I don't know what to do anymore,' he said.

I could see that, but there was something else as well. He sounded really angry, and as he spoke Carly seemed to slump even deeper into the despair which her chair only partially managed to prop up.

'How come you're so angry?' I asked him.

'Angry?' he said, in an angry voice. 'I'm not angry.'

'You sound angry.'

'Do I? Well, I don't mean to.'

I didn't necessarily believe that. I thought he meant to sound angry, despite his protestations. In any case I thought it was a pretty confusing signal to give to his daughter, who looked like she was in desperate need of clarity on all kinds of levels.

'You say that you don't mean to sound angry, but you still sound angry to me.'

Now he frowned, his face having clearly decided to follow the tone of voice. 'Well, I'm not.'

'Actually, I think you pretty clearly are angry now, except now you're predominantly angry at me for saying that you're angry all the time.'

'I will say this one — more — time,' he said, labouring each word. 'I — am — not — angry.'

Even if the stakes had been much lower I wouldn't have let that one go, but with his daughter's life on the line I sure as hell wasn't going to back away.

'Look, Tom, I'm not trying to have a go. Seriously, I'm not. But I think that you *are* angry, and for some reason you don't seem to want to admit it even though it's painfully obvious to everyone else in the room. So the reason I'm badgering you about it is that I think maybe one of the things Carly struggles with is that in this family there are a whole lot of suppressed feelings bumping about and a huge mismatch between words and behaviour. That can be confusing for kids, and it can make them feel anxious. I think you'd agree that probably the last thing your daughter needs right now is to have to try and decode what you're actually saying.'

He looked at me for a long moment. 'I guess so.'

It was a small admission, but I was happy with that.

'I wouldn't be surprised if you were angry with Carly, because you're probably really worried about her, and often when dads get worried that seems to come out sounding a little angry. The thing is, though, that she doesn't need you to be angry with her. She needs to know that you're on her side and that you're going to stick by her no matter what it takes until she beats this thing.'

'She knows that already,' he said, although his tone remained snippy. He still wasn't getting what he was doing and, worse, he was taking more notice of how he felt than how *she* felt. Suddenly I began to understand a little more the lack of connection between the two of them,

'I think there's a lot of history here, and a lot of worry on both sides – and most of all I think that everyone is hunkered down behind their own walls waiting for the other one to come out first. I think what we need to do here is work out how to get out from the bunkers and get to know each other a little more.'

'Are you saying that the reason Carly doesn't eat is because of me?'

I shrugged. 'Not completely. From my experience, and from what I know about the research in this area it's likely to be a number of things, but I think you might well be a part of it, yeah.'

'So it's all my fault?'

'No, not all of it. Maybe not even part of it – but you're her dad, and if you can't influence her then no one can.'

He paused for a moment, trying to work out if what I'd just said was a compliment or an insult. In the end I don't think he was sure, so gave up. 'So what do I do, then?'

'Sing,' I said, raising my arms theatrically.

'What?' Tom muttered, frowning.

'Nah, nah, I was just jokin'. How about we just talk for a bit?'

Carly giggled.

It was a fine start.

Families where eating disorders are more likely

These are a list of some of the family factors or dynamics that tend to be present when children have an eating disorder. Not all of these factors need to be present. Some will and some won't in most cases. Researchers are still arguing about the exact nature of how these things directly affect the development of eating disorders, but I think it's a fairly widespread assumption amongst the clever people who've spent the past four decades studying this stuff that it is not good to have families where:

◊ girls have little or no contact with their fathers

◊ the parents are over-controlling and over-protective

◊ the parents are psychologically manipulative (eg, they repeatedly bring up past mistakes or stop talking to their kids when they have done something to upset them)

◊ the parents create a high level of dependency in their children

◊ there are low levels of intimacy and affection

◊ girls feel that their parents have no interest in, or connection with, their daily lives

◊ appearance is emphasized

◊ there are high levels of stress within the family

◊ there are high levels of conflict between parents

◊ there are high levels of conflict between parents and children

◊ there is emotional, sexual, and/or physical abuse.

Now, I know what you're probably thinking: exactly what does 'high levels of conflict' mean? Conflict is, after all, pretty bloody normal when you have a teenager living in the house, or even a pre-teen for that matter. So how much is too much?

Unfortunately, I have no answer for you on that one. No one does. It's likely that a complex web of these factors will exist, and some of them might cause an eating disorder, while others might be the effect of an eating disorder on the family. Whatever the case, it doesn't really matter — all you need to know is that there's now a pretty big pile of science which says those things are things to watch out for.

What you can do?

All this means that there are some really important things you can do to provide your daughter with the kind of home environment that is most likely to prevent her from developing these kinds of issues.

◊ Prioritize taking the time to talk to her about her life and what's going on. Make sure she knows that you're there, and that you're interested.

◊ Get rid of bathroom scales.

◊ Never criticize or tease her about her weight.

◊ Don't talk about what you like about her appearance — talk about what you like about her as a person.

◊ Be careful about the kinds of magazines and television shows you let into your home, and remember that you need to start thinking about that stuff from when she's little.

◊ Build a good relationship with her mum, and show that every day.

◊ If you and her mum are getting into conflict all the time, get it sorted as soon as you can. Get help to do this if you need to.

◊ Make her feel loved by showing her that she's loved.

◊ Make her understand that you love her for who she is. Love who she is, not who you'd like her to be.

◊ Tell her that you believe in her.

◊ Give her the freedom and autonomy to make decisions for herself, and then support those decisions wherever and whenever you can.

◊ Help her to learn to solve problems as they arrive.

◊ Keep the stress in the house down as much as you can.

◊ Encourage her to talk about her feelings.

◊ If she is feeling anxious, or depressed, or having trouble coping, keep talking with her about these things. If you feel really worried, seek some appropriately qualified help for her.

◊ When you do have conflict — and you will — make sure that you sort it out as soon as you can. You can't help getting into conflict with her from time to time, just make sure it isn't all the time.

◊ Encourage healthy eating, not dieting.

◊ Eat as a family at the dinner table with no television on in the background.

As you can see, it's important that you foster a sense of autonomy and acceptance in your daughter. The more she feels accepted and supported, the less likely she is to develop the kinds of emotional problems which might lead her to try to cope by controlling what she eats.

It's also very important that you don't ever tease her about her weight, or try to regulate or control her eating. In one longitudinal study, where researchers followed 216 newborns and their parents from birth to 11 years of age, the girls whose fathers tried to regulate their eating and weight were most at risk of developing an eating disorder.

So don't.

Ever.

Another important finding goes against what you might expect. Most dads would probably think that commenting on how 'skinny and horrible' the stick-like models on television look would be a good thing. The line of reasoning being that if your daughter knows that you think skinny is not attractive, then she won't feel any pressure to lose weight. Interestingly, some researchers have found that the degree that parents commented on physical appearance of television characters was associated with disordered eating — except the real kicker here was that this effect was seen regardless of whether the comments were positive or negative. So what this suggests is that talking a lot about appearance, either positively or negatively, can cause problems.

So, as much as you possibly can, try to convey to her that what matters is not how you look, but who you are. The way you can probably do this most effectively is by not commenting on how people in the media look, but what you think about who they are as people.

If there was a golden rule for providing the best environment to 'immunize' your daughter against developing eating problems and a preoccupation with thinness and dieting, it would seem to be this: model healthy living and eating, and aim for low conflict and high acceptance.

If you do that, then you're doing the best that you can.

What to do if you think she may have a problem

If you become concerned that your daughter may have a problem, the first most important rule, as ever, is don't panic. The worst thing you can do is go charging in, so take a moment and get yourself in the right space. You need to be calm, measured, and considered when you talk to her. Once you've got yourself into the right headspace, I'd suggest the following:

◊ Be direct.

◊ Tell her that you're concerned about her, and outline what your specific concerns are.

◊ Listen to her response, and be understanding, empathetic, and patient. She might be scared as well.

◊ Don't belittle her fears, or get angry or frustrated.

◊ Learn as much as you can about eating disorders. There are loads of informative and helpful websites on the internet.

◊ If you are still concerned, get professional help. This is a specialist area, so make sure you talk to someone who works in this area and not a general counsellor. The best place to start if you are completely lost is by telephoning your local hospital, because they should be able to refer you on to the specialist team in your area.

Just as we know a lot more about the likely causes of eating disorders amongst young women, we also know a lot more about how to treat sufferers as well. In most developed nations there are now specialist treatment centres for young people suffering from an eating disorder, with options usually ranging from outpatient treatment to hospital admissions. The help is out there: you just need to reach out and find it if you need it.

Tips on
Body image and eating disorders

☆ Girls can show an unhealthy concern with body image and weight from a very young age, but the early teen years (11–14 years) seem to be a time of particular risk.

☆ There is a suggestion that talking about appearance (whether approving or critical) can contribute to body image problems.

☆ Be aware of the possible warning signs of eating disorders.

☆ The most important thing to understand is that there are a number of things you can do to create the home environment which is most likely to prevent her from developing these kinds of problems.

☆ If you are concerned, talk to her about your concerns, and get professional help.

20

Depression, anxiety, and self-harm

Not the most cheery of chapter headings, is it? I tried to find something a bit more upbeat and funny, but it's hard to be upbeat and funny when you're talking about depression, anxiety, and self-harm.

'Did you hear the one about the anxious girl, the depressed girl, and the girl who used to cut herself with razor blades?'

Hard to find a punch line for that one.

So rather than trying to be upbeat and funny, I thought I'd be straight-up about all this stuff.

Whilst boys also suffer from all three of these issues, girls tend to experience all three in far greater numbers. The reason for this may be that girls, as a general rule, tend to have more of a negative view of themselves in terms of achievement, self-worth, and their physical appearance than boys, and this might predispose them to these kinds of issues.

Whatever the root causes for this, all that really matters to the fathers of girls is that girls seem to be more likely than boys to experience depression or anxiety, and to deliberately try to harm themselves.

All of which clearly means that this is stuff you need to know about.

Depression and anxiety

Depression and anxiety are like the two evil twins of adolescent mental health. They affect large numbers of young people, particularly girls, and they often seem to appear together. It seems that the common thread between these two diagnoses is an underlying tendency to experience negative feelings, which is often expressed as both depressive and anxious feelings.

It also seems that the early teenage years are a particularly vulnerable time for the onset of depression, but the good news is that, if picked up early and adequate help is given, the research indicates that teenagers are particularly responsive to treatment and the long-term picture is very good. So it seems pretty obvious that it's good to know what the signs and symptoms of depression are so that, if you do become aware there might be a problem, you can get in quick and do something about it.

Possible signs of *depression* in teenagers are:

◊ feelings of sadness or hopelessness

◊ irritability or anger, particularly extreme sensitivity to criticism

◊ tearfulness and frequent crying

◊ loss of interest in activities

◊ withdrawal from friends and/or family

◊ agitation and restlessness

◊ lack of enthusiasm for life

◊ feeling tired

◊ difficulty concentrating

◊ changes in eating and sleeping habits.

Possible signs of *anxiety* in teenagers are:

◊ feeling anxious or stressed

◊ avoiding social contacts

◇ avoiding situations where they are 'on display'

◇ specific fears

◇ panic attacks (heartbeat racing, increased breathing, sweating, feelings of panic)

◇ changes in eating or sleeping habits

◇ tearfulness or upset

◇ irritability.

As you can see there is quite a lot of overlap between the two, and it doesn't really matter which list you decide that symptom might be from. All that matters is that you notice it, and then you do something about it. We'll go over the what-you-should-do part of all this in a moment. Just for now, though, remember that whilst none of these signs and symptoms is definitive: you should consider them as little red flags. When you see them, you'd be well advised to spend a little more time checking out with your daughter how she's doing.

Self-harm

This is a pretty frightening one for any parent. We all know stories of families who have lost children through suicide, either through direct experience or through the media, but for every death there are far more kids who engage in various acts of self-harm, from cutting and burning through to ingesting poisons. As with most things knowledge is power, and so understanding what might be underlying these behaviours is fundamentally important.

It probably won't surprise you to learn that there has been quite a lot of research looking at this issue, and it might surprise you even less to know that the picture seems to be complex. There is no straight line from having the thoughts to committing self-harming acts, and it seems that a variety of factors interact in fairly complex ways, and that girls seem to experience thoughts of self-harm, and indeed to act on these thoughts, in quite distinct ways.

The gender paradox

The gender paradox refers to the fact that, whilst more girls than boys attempt suicide, fewer girls die than boys. The reason for this is that boys tend to utilize more highly lethal methods, such as carbon monoxide poisoning in vehicles, hanging, or firearms. Girls tend to use less lethal methods, such as drug overdoses.

Why do kids self-harm?

In a very large international study, a total of 30,477 students aged between 14 and 17 from seven countries (Australia, Belgium, England, Hungary, Ireland, the Netherlands, and Norway) were asked to fill out an anonymous self-report questionnaire which asked them questions about self-harming behaviour in the past year, and also over the course of their lifetime. The researchers were trying to understand why teenagers engage in these kinds of behaviours. The two most commonly reported reasons were 'wanted to get relief from a terrible state of mind' and 'wanted to die'. It seemed that the underlying motive tended to be driven by both a cry of pain motive and a cry for help motive.

The majority of teenagers in the study reported at least one cry of pain motive ('to die', 'to punish myself', and 'to get relief from a terrible state of mind') and one cry for help motive ('to show someone how desperate I was feeling', 'to frighten someone', 'to get my own back on someone', 'to find out whether someone really loved me', and 'to get some attention'). The girls in the study tended to report more reasons than the males, and older girls reported more reasons that were about a cry for help. A possible explanation for the observation that girls reported more reasons than boys might be that they have a greater need to explain what happened, and to communicate their distress, or possibly that they have a more complex understanding of their motives than boys.

In any case, what is important for all of us to know is that it seems pretty clear that these kinds of behaviours are more complex than just a cry for help alone.

Risk factors and warning signs

It's pretty clear, then, that this stuff is driven by some pretty powerful feelings, which leads to the next obvious question: what exactly produces those feelings? Why do girls feel like they want to hurt themselves, or feel the need to cry out for help? It seems that there are a number of factors which might place kids at more risk of self-harm. When you look at this list, though, it's important to understand that these are only *possible* risk factors. None of these things are definitive. They are just things which, if she experiences them, *might* place her at a greater risk of having thoughts of self-harm:

◊ psychiatric illness (eg, depression)

◊ socio-economic disadvantage

◊ substance abuse (lowers inhibitions and, in some cases — alcohol, for instance — acts as a depressant)

◊ childhood experiences of abuse

◊ living in separated families

◊ parental mental-health issues

◊ conflict with parents

◊ stressful and/or traumatic life events (eg, trouble at school or a relationship break-up)

◊ poor problem-solving abilities

◊ low self-efficacy (the belief you can achieve things)

◊ having lots of negative thoughts about self

◊ having lots of negative feelings.

As with all lists like this, they can be a little alarming. What's important to understand, though, is that these factors are not prescriptive. Just because your daughter has a conflicted relationship with her parents does not mean that she will have thoughts of self-harm. All it means is that she has an increased risk of developing those kinds of thoughts and behaviours. Remember, too, that what you have to keep in mind when you're thinking about 'research' is that the general trends can be useful to know, but what's more important is how *your* girl is actually doing. The good news is that you can do something about almost all of the items on that list. Have another look at the list now.

Do you see what I mean? Obviously there are going to be some things you can't have an impact on, like being separated, but everything else is up for grabs. Everything else you can influence — maybe not fix, but certainly influence. We'll come back to this in a moment or so, but first let's look at possible warning signs.

The following are possible warning signs that a teenager might be suicidal. Bear in mind, though, that none of these are definitive signs, and many of them are quite normal in teenagers who tend to be 'a bit up and down' at the best of times. The golden rule here is trust your instincts, and if you're worried then get some professional help. Warning signs include:

◊ talking or writing about suicide

◊ changes in eating or sleeping patterns

◊ significant change in behaviour

◊ a sudden 'improvement' in depressed mood (the reason for this is that once they decide to kill themselves, people often experience a paradoxical lifting of their mood as they can feel they finally have an option)

◊ loss of interest in previously enjoyable activities

◊ withdrawal from friends and family

◊ giving away possessions

◇ stressful events (eg, relationship break-ups)

◇ alcohol and drug use

◇ apologizing for past behaviour.

Again, none of these things in and of themselves mean that your daughter is suicidal, but they're the kinds of things you should keep an eye out for, and not ignore if you see them.

What to do if you're worried

There are a number of things you can do if you're worried about your daughter. It might be that she seems depressed, or she might have started showing some of the warning signs listed above, or you might have discovered that she is deliberately cutting herself, or harming herself in some other way.

◇ Keep calm. If you panic, all you'll succeed in doing is clouding the water.

◇ Talk to her about your concerns and be direct. Don't shy away from the big issue: use the S-word if that's what you are worried about.

◇ Ask her questions, don't lecture. She doesn't need you to go on at her; she almost certainly needs you to listen to her explain how she feels and why.

◇ Take her concerns seriously. It might not seem like a big deal from where you're sitting, but things can seem very different when you're young. Make sure she knows that you take her seriously.

◇ Make sure she knows that you are there for her, and that you'll do whatever it takes to help her get happy again.

◇ Make the immediate environment as safe as you can by removing anything obvious she could use to hurt or harm herself.

◊ If in doubt, get professional help. This might be a psychologist or a counsellor, or even your family doctor. If you have no idea where to go for help, just telephone your local hospital and they will almost certainly be able to put you in touch with the people you need to speak to.

More than any other time, this is when you need to keep a level head. There are few issues as scary as this, but you have to keep your own worries in check. Your focus needs to be on finding out what is going on with her, and then doing whatever you need to do to help her get back on solid ground again.

Tips on
Depression, anxiety, and self-harm

☆ Depression and anxiety affect a large number of young people, particularly young women, and the early teenage years are a particularly vulnerable time.

☆ Teenagers who self-harm seem to be driven by different motives, but these usually centre on a 'cry of pain' (ie, to die, to punish herself, to get relief from a terrible state of mind) and a 'cry for help' (ie, to frighten someone, to get their own back, to find out if someone really loves them, to get some attention).

☆ If you are worried, learn about the early warning signs, talk to her about your concerns, and get professional help if you need to.

21

Every dad's nightmare: sex, drugs, and parties

There's a reason why fathers of teenage girls don't like boyfriends: it's because we all used to be one. We remember what it was like when we were that age, and what we spent a tremendous amount of time thinking about — which is why you know that, no matter how polite, well-mannered, considerate, and generally pleasant he might seem, pretty much his sole focus is on getting lucky with your daughter. You know it, and he knows it. No one speaks of it, because that would be too weird, but you know what he's thinking, and planning, and generally scheming.

It's enough to make a Quaker get a firearms licence.

So here's the thing: none of us want our kids to have sexual relationships. Ever. We just don't. The problem is that this is yet another one of those bits of parenting where what we want and what they want are two different things. Gone are the days when, like Galileo the famous Italian astronomer, you could simply put your daughters in a convent. Galileo actually put both his daughters, Virginia and Livia, into a convent in Arcetri, and they remained there for the rest of their lives. So despite the fact that, as I said earlier, he fell offside with the Pope for saying that the Earth revolved around the sun, and then spent the last part of his life under house arrest, with a painful hernia and completely blind, at least he didn't have to worry about boys.

Oh, for the good old days of the 16th century, eh?

For the rest of us, where convent life isn't an option, we just need to get over the fact that our kids are going to have a sexual life, and then do the very best we can to make sure we support them to conduct it in a responsible and healthy way.

What predicts earlier sexual activity?

It's pretty evident that a lot of scientists have children, because there's been quite a lot of research internationally looking at just this issue. This is probably why we haven't found a cure for cancer yet, or fixed global warming — all the scientists are far more interested in finding out what things are more likely to make their kids engage in sexual behaviours. Not surprisingly, they've found a few things which should give us all pause for thought. One Scottish study of 4,379 teenagers found that the kids reporting early sexual intercourse were more likely to be female, not living with both biological parents, had more spending money, had poor family relationships, and weren't engaged in school.

Except it gets even more interesting, and more relevant to you, because researchers also found that, not only was the relationship with the teenager and the parent more important than the parents' relationship with each other, but having an absent father increases the risk of a girl engaging in early sexual behaviour. Even more interesting still is the fact that girls in particular seem to respond very positively to having fathers who are actively engaged in their lives and having families where there are regular family activities, such as eating meals together.

Bottom line: dads can potentially play a *huge* role in helping their daughters deal with their emerging sexuality.

Aside from convents, what are the options?

Just the one: talk to her. There is absolutely no way around this one. You can get through the basic puberty talk by giving her books, or palming her off on her mum, but you have to talk to her about sex. You just have to. The research shows very clearly that girls who have an open and supportive relationship with their fathers in particular are more likely to wait longer to have sex, and to use safe sex practices when they do. So here's my take on how to do all that.

◊ *Get educated.* Make sure you know the facts yourself. You need to get familiar with the nuts and bolts so you don't sound like a stumbling idiot.

◊ *It's not a one-off deal.* This is not something you do once and then cross off the list. Like so many of the big issues, it's something you need to come back to as many times as she needs to.

◊ *Sex is a big deal.* It's important that she understands that sex is a big deal. You don't want to give her some kind of complex, but it's important that she needs to get that sex is a big step, and that it isn't something she should do without really thinking about it.

◊ *Strong emotions.* She needs to have a way to understand the strong emotions that will come with sexual attraction. It's normal to feel these things, but she also needs to be able to step back from the feelings and think carefully about the choices she is making.

◊ *No means no.* You need to talk to her about risky situations and what she can do if she finds herself being pressured for sex. She needs to know that she has an absolute right to say no at any stage, and that the boy needs to respect that.

◊ *Ask her questions.* Give her plenty of space to tell you what she thinks about all this. It's a discussion, not a lecture — and you need to remember that if you want her to talk to you about what is going on in her life.

You just need to keep in mind that if you want her to be safe and healthy, then the best way to achieve that is through making her feel secure and good about herself. You can't afford to stick your head in the sand over this one. You can't simply throw a few pamphlets at her and leave her to it. If you're a single dad you'll have absolutely no option, but if you're living with her mum it might feel like the best thing is just to leave all that girly stuff to them.

But it isn't.

So don't.

Alcohol and drugs

You only need to watch the evening news to see that alcohol and drug use is a growing problem. Even worse, go down to the centre of almost any major city in the developed world sometime around midnight on a Saturday and you'll see stuff that will make your toes curl. The police are regularly picking up young women so completely intoxicated they don't even know where they are.

And that's without us even getting into the whole scourge of drugs like methamphetamines which seem to know no social barriers. That stuff will take the rich kids and the poor kids without discrimination. It's the equal opportunity drug, because it will fuck up anyone who's stupid enough, or naïve enough, to ask it for a dance.

So against this fairly scary backdrop, what's a poor dad to do? Again, as with so many complex problems, the answers are fairly simple. Here's my standard advice when it comes to dealing with alcohol and drugs.

◊ Talk to her about drugs whenever the opportunity arises (eg, watching something on TV or at the movies, reading newspapers). Obviously you don't want to harp on about this stuff, but if the chance presents itself to have a conversation then take it.

◊ Don't get all preachy — that's generally counterproductive. However, it's good to tell her about your values and beliefs in relation to drug use.

◊ Make sure that what you're telling her about drugs and alcohol is accurate. If you don't know, get on the internet and find out.

◊ Ask her to explain her views on alcohol and drugs.

◊ Keep calm and keep talking if she tells you that she is using, or has used, drugs.

◊ Have conversations about peer pressure, and give her strategies to deal with this pressure (eg, she can say things like 'I can't, because my dad drug-tests me').

◊ Make sure she understands that, whatever happens, she can always come to you for advice — it is really important that she know this.

◊ Don't get drunk or use drugs. How can you expect her to take you seriously if she sees you using drugs or getting drunk? So don't.

These are also some *possible* signs that your daughter might be using drugs. None of these are definitive, so don't panic if she comes home with bloodshot eyes, for instance, because she might just be tired. Still, these are some things to maybe keep an eye out for:

◊ drugs or drug paraphernalia on her or in her room (if you don't know what this stuff looks like, use Google Image Search and get familiar with it)

◊ the smell of drugs on her (a sneaky thing to do is give her a hug when she gets home after a party, although remember she may have been around drugs but not using them)

◊ bloodshot eyes, although some teenagers use eye drops to keep their eyes clear

◊ staggering, difficulty focusing, or slurred speech

◊ sudden change in mood or behaviour

◊ loss of interest in activities she used to enjoy

◊ sudden change of friends

◊ school performance deteriorates

◊ secretive phone calls

◊ money or other items going missing at home

◊ failing a home drug test — these are now available over the internet, so parents can test their kids to see if they are telling the truth.

And what can you do if you suspect there is a problem?

◊ Don't panic. Most of all don't panic, because that almost always ends badly.

◊ Don't come in with all guns blazing. If you do this, she'll most likely respond by getting indignant and defensive.

◊ Choose a calm, peaceful moment when you have the best chance of engaging her in a conversation.

◊ Be direct about your concerns without being accusatory.
 — Good: *'I know that you've been using marijuana, and so we need to talk about that.'*
 — Not so good: *'I know you've been getting stoned, so don't lie to me.'*

◊ Listen to her, don't simply lecture her. She's more likely to talk if she believes you are interested in hearing what she has to say.

◊ Remember that you have rights just as much as she has. Principally, you have the right to live in a drug-free home.

◊ If she says there's no problem but you think there is, call someone for help. Drug and alcohol treatment centres are listed in the phone directory, and they are a good place to go for information, advice, and support.

There's no silver bullet here other than good old-fashioned common sense. Another of my books, *Before Your Teenagers Drive You Crazy, Read This!*, contains a whole chapter on the issue of substance abuse and teenagers.

Parties

Parties are a stressful time in any parent's life. Your daughter is going to want to go to them without doubt, and there's nothing you can really do about that. Besides, even if you could you shouldn't. These first starry forays into the social world will be where she learns some important lessons about herself and the world. This is the beginning of her own life, and she needs to get out there and practise.

The problem for us, of course, is that parties are a source of abject terror. When it's after midnight and she's still not home, there isn't a chance in Hell of you sleeping. You'll tell yourself that it's fine over and over in your head as you lie in bed wound tighter than a monkey's tail, listening intently for the noise of an approaching vehicle, or the most reassuring sound in the world: the sound of a key in the front door.

When it comes to parties, I think the best party rules I've ever come across were told to me by a Police Youth Aid Officer. He is a very sensible bloke who'd worked in all areas of the police, including guarding the prime minister at one point on the Diplomatic Protection Squad, and on the Armed Offender's Squad. He was a man with his feet squarely on the ground, and utterly capable in all kinds of ways. These were the rules he used with his kids, and I share them now with you.

1 If you're going to a party, I have to know who's holding it and where it will be.

2 I will drop you off a block away from the house so your friends don't have to see you getting out of your dad's car.

3 You can take a six-pack of beer, and that's all you're allowed to drink.

4 No drugs. At all. Ever.

5 At the agreed time I will park in the same spot, a block away from the house, and you will meet me there so no one has to see you getting into my car.

6 If you aren't there on time I will park in front of the house, turn the hazard lights on, and walk into the house making more fuss and noise than you ever dreamed possible. I will find you, and will march you out to my car in front of all your friends.

7 Stick to the rules and we'll have no problems, and you'll go to lots of parties.

8 Break the rules and that's the end of parties for quite some time.

He never had any problems with his kids at parties, and I'm not surprised. I think these rules are bloody great. There's plenty of room in there for kids to go out and have fun, but enough structure so they can't get too far out of their depth. To be sure, there are always going to be unexpected situations that you can't plan for, but in my view these rules are the kind of thing you should be using to let your kids go out there and do the things that teenagers do, whilst at the same time putting enough structure around it so they don't run out there and do the things that teenagers do.

Have an emergency code word

Something else that is helpful to have is a secret code word, which only you and she know, that she can use if she feels like she's in too deep and wants someone to come get her. Sometimes she might be out with her friends and they are all wanting to go off somewhere that she feels isn't safe. In that situation it can be hard for her to pull out without looking like a baby in front of her friends. If she can call you, on the pretext that she has to check in at a certain time, and slip in the secret code word or phrase (eg, the cat's name, or asking if her light is turned off in her room), then you can tell her that she has to come home right then and there and go pick her up. This lets her save face, and gets her home where she's safe.

Tips on

Sex, drugs, and parties

☆ If you're in her life, and you're talking to her about sex, then she's more likely to wait longer before becoming sexually active, and to practise safe sex when she does.

☆ This means you do have to talk to her about sex, and not just once, but throughout the whole trip.

☆ Alcohol and drugs are everywhere, so she's going to be around this stuff.

☆ Educate yourself about them, and talk to her about them as well.

☆ Parties are also a fact of life, so establish some clear, reasonable rules and expectations.

☆ Have an emergency code word she can use if she wants you to come get her.

22

Bad girls

We've talked about the Dunedin Multidisciplinary Health and Development Study (DMDHDS) earlier, remember? It was the one where they've spent the past 37 years following 1,037 people through their whole lives to see what happens along the way. There were a couple of things I left out. One of them was that, if you were to go visit them, sandwiched in between the Dental School and the Zoology Department — in a small two-storey building which seems oddly nondescript considering the magnitude of what they've been busy doing for coming up to four decades — then you must make sure you go to a wee café just across from them on the one-way system on Cumberland Street.

They make really great date scones.

The second, and slightly more relevant, thing is that amongst all the many different facets of human development they've been studying, one of them is the criminal and delinquent behaviour girls get up to. In 2001, some of the researchers published a book called *Sex Differences in Antisocial Behaviour*, which neatly summarized everything they'd learned so far. For people like me who spend a lot of time working with kids who commit crimes and get into trouble, it's a fascinating read and provides a truly unique window into the world of teenage delinquency.

Having said that, it is a bit scientific, what with the graphs and statistics and all, so to make it easier for you I thought I'd summarize the main findings here, because reading research papers is a little heavy going, even for people who enjoy that kind of thing. I haven't covered everything they've found, because not all of it is relevant to the business of parenting, but there are quite a few things that are directly relevant, and I think quite helpful to know. Forewarned is forearmed after all.

In keeping with the fact that this is a book for dads, I'm going to present their findings addressing major questions you might have with key bullet-point answers. I know bullet points can get a bit annoying if you have too many, but there was just too much good stuff and I didn't want to leave anything out.

Are there sex differences in the levels of antisocial behaviour?

◊ A very small group of girls commit the majority of offences.

◊ Girls' offending is generally less antisocial, and so they get in less trouble with the authorities than boys.

◊ Girls and boys are most similar in their drug- and alcohol-related offending.

◊ Girls' and boys' antisocial behaviour is closest around age 15, after which boys' offending becomes more serious.

◊ More boys are diagnosed with serious behaviour issues than girls across the lifespan, *except* during very early adolescence when the incidence of girls' serious behaviour increases to narrow the gap more than at any other time.

◊ The fact that girls physically appear older may help push a girl into antisocial behaviour by making her, or older kids, think she is ready to join in with their antisocial behaviour.

Are there sex differences in physical violence and partner abuse?

◊ Girls are less physically violent than boys at every age and in every setting except . . .

◇ Girls matched or exceeded boys when it came to violence against intimate partners.

◇ As we talked about earlier in Chapter 18, this violence was serious and was not simply violence committed in acts of self-defence.

When does antisocial behaviour begin?

◇ Estimates of the age of onset vary widely between different studies.

◇ What we do know is that antisocial behaviour typically begins about three to five years before the first conviction.

◇ Beginning antisocial behaviour in adulthood is extremely rare.

Are girls vulnerable to the same risk factors as boys?

◇ Antisocial behaviour in girls and boys is predicted by the same kinds of risk factors.

◇ Risk factors include family problems, lower intelligence, hyperactivity, and poor self-control.

◇ Girls generally seem to experience fewer risk factors than boys, and in particular they have lower rates of hyperactivity, peer problems, and the kinds of neurological issues which predict antisocial behaviour.

Can personality differences explain the lower rates of antisocial behaviour in girls?

◇ It seems they do.

◇ Specific personality traits (ie, negative feelings and low self-control) are associated with antisocial behaviour in both girls and boys.

◇ Girls have much fewer of these traits, and this seems to be why girls engage in less antisocial behaviour.

How do other mental-health issues have an impact on antisocial behaviour?

◊ In 90% of cases where young people have serious behaviour problems, there will be a co-existing problem such as anxiety, depression, substance abuse, ADHD, and/or reading difficulties.

◊ Girls and boys are very similar in this respect.

◊ The only difference seems to be that for girls depression seems to *follow* serious behaviour problems rather than precede it.

What effect does antisocial behaviour in teenagers have on their adult lives?

◊ For both girls and boys the long-term consequences of persistent antisocial behaviour can be serious, although the effects differ slightly.

◊ Young men are more likely to have later problems at work, with substance abuse, and with the law.

◊ Young women tend to have more problems with relationships, depression, self-harm, and poor physical health.

Is there any relationship between dropkick boyfriends and antisocial behaviour?

◊ Girls with an antisocial history are more likely to hook up with boys from the wrong side of the tracks.

◊ They are also more likely to form relationships with boys who have little education, are poor readers, and who are violent towards them.

◊ Antisocial girls, having met an antisocial boy, are more likely to have babies at a younger age.

◊ One of the key deciders over whether a girl continues her antisocial behaviour into adulthood is who she forms a relationship with. Bad boys lead to more trouble, and good boys make for happier endings.

◊ The problem is that bad girls get stuck in a vicious cycle where hooking up with bad boys is the most likely outcome.

How many stop and how many keep going?

◊ The good news is that the vast majority of girls (99% in fact) stop their antisocial behaviour after adolescence.

◊ Only 1 in a 100 girls will go on to continue their antisocial behaviour after adolescence.

◊ Phew.

There's a lot to take in there, so you might need to read it a couple of times. The big message which comes out of all this for the fathers of girls is that there's actually plenty of good news. Whilst the impacts of antisocial behaviour are just as bad for girls as they are for boys — albeit in slightly different ways — girls appear to engage in a lot less serious antisocial behaviour, and they generally get into a lot less trouble. Not only that, but the biggest and best-est, most hope-giving-est point of the whole lot is that 99% of girls leave all that stuff behind them when they enter young adulthood.

I've said it before, and I'll say it again: phew.

What to do if your girl gets in trouble

Now, despite the fact that girls are less likely to cause the kinds of trouble that will bring them into conflict with the powers that be, it does still happen. Remember that her brain is still a work in progress, and so sometimes she might make decisions that seem just plain . . . well . . . dumb. It happens. The big thing is to make sure that when it does happen you do the right thing. I've been working with young offenders for quite a long time now, all the way from shoplifters to killers, and over that time I think I've developed a pretty good idea of what you should do, and just as importantly what you shouldn't do.

For what it's worth, here's my two cents' worth on the best way to respond when your girl comes unstuck.

◊ *Don't panic*

This one is important, because what you need most when the proverbial waste material has hit the air-circulating device is a cool head. You need to stop, take a breath, and think before you decide what to do next.

◊ *Don't get too angry*

You are going to get angry, that's a given, in fact I recommend it — just don't get too angry. You need to get at least a little bit angry so that she knows this is a big deal, and that you disapprove of what she did. The last thing you want her to think is that you don't really mind. So be angry, just don't go ballistic. As a guide I'd suggest a Barack Obama angry (cool, measured, and targeted), not a George W Bush angry (crazy, ill-considered, rabid, likely to go off and invade random countries without really thinking it through).

◊ *Let her feel the consequences fully*

You must not protect her from the consequences of her actions. Don't ride in and save her, and don't bail her out. You don't want to be the parent arguing for lighter consequences if she's done something wrong. Feeling the consequences of our bad decisions is how we all learn, so don't cheat her out of the chance to learn from her mistakes.

◊ *Seek wise counsel, not clever counsel*

If you are at the point where you need to get a lawyer, be careful who you choose. There are some very good youth advocates out there, but there are also some crap ones. Remember that lawyers primarily want to get their client off. That's their job. However, the lawyer's definition of winning and what's best for your daughter may be two different things. Getting her off on some technicality is not winning — it's the worst kind of losing.

◇ *Model respect*
You must always model respect for the system. Never bad-mouth authority figures in front of her. Ever. Don't run down her teacher, her school, the police, or the courts. These institutions and people are often the only thing that stands between us and chaos.

◇ *Compassion is good, idiot compassion not so much*
The term 'idiot compassion' was first coined by the Buddhist monk Trungpa Rinpoche. He made the very wise point that whilst it is a very good thing to have compassion for people, especially people who make mistakes, it is not a good thing to have compassion for people who keep making the same mistake over and over. That's not compassion; it's idiot compassion. You should have compassion for your daughter when she makes mistakes, the more the better, but if she keeps making the same mistake over and over, and ignores or rejects offers of help, then you need to make sure you're not showering her with idiot compassion.

Trouble comes to us all, and most of us probably got into trouble when we were young as well. You often don't set out to cause trouble, it just somehow finds you. So it isn't what's happened that you should be most concerned about. What's done is done. What really matters is how you respond. It's not about what she's done so much as it is about what you do next.

Learning from others' mistakes

I'm a great believer in mistakes, because I've generally learned a lot more from those then I ever have from my successes. Along that same line, I've also seen plenty of parents make mistakes with their daughters that we can all learn from. Obviously it would be nice if none of us screwed things up with our kids, but we all do from time to time. The big thing is simply to learn from it and move on.

So in that light, let me give you three cautionary tales.

Nicole, aged 15, assaulting a teacher

Nicole had been having problems at school for quite a while. She was lippy, snotty, and generally pissy with her teachers on an almost daily basis. She was pretty, and popular, and seemed to think the school rules were beneath her. At the beginning of an English class, she had been talking to her friend when the teacher — a young woman who was new to teaching, and with whom Nicole had already had run-ins on several occasions — told her to be quiet. She told the teacher to get fucked. The teacher asked her to leave the class. She refused. The teacher then walked up to her and demanded that she leave. She did, but not before she'd slapped the teacher in the face.

What her parents did

Nicole's mum and dad came in with guns blazing. They said that, while they didn't condone what their daughter had done, they did think Nicole had been provoked. In their view, and by Nicole's own account, the teacher had used an aggressive tone and had intruded on Nicole's personal space, making her feel both cornered and humiliated in front of her peers. Her response had been instinctive and simply a reaction to feeling threatened. They said that they thought it only right that the teacher apologize to their daughter and receive some further instruction on how to effectively manage her class without the bullying techniques she clearly was using at present.

What they should have done

1 Immediately make it clear to Nicole that her behaviour was completely unacceptable.

2 Immediately withdraw all privileges of any kind.

3 Contact the school and arrange a meeting as soon as possible.

4 At that meeting ensure that Nicole apologized to the teacher for her appalling behaviour.

5 Negotiate with the school, and the teacher, an appropriately severe punishment.

Tanya, aged 16, vandalism

While Tanya was out with some friends one Friday night, they had all decided that it would be terribly amusing to throw some rocks through a service station window after the person behind the counter had refused to sell them cigarettes. They hadn't managed to break the window, but they did crack the glass, which then had to be replaced at huge expense to the owner. The police caught the girls as they were walking away, giggling and shrieking over the highly amusing trick they'd just played.

What her dad did

From the very start, Tanya's dad took the view that his daughter had been simply 'caught up in an impulsive act', and what's more this act was largely driven by an older girl in the group. While acknowledging that his daughter had been part of the group, he did not accept that she was as culpable as the other members of the group. He duly employed a very clever lawyer, who successfully argued the case that, because it was impossible to prove who had thrown the rocks, Tanya could not be held responsible. The lawyer won, and Tanya was not charged, did not have to pay any reparation, and could happily go on with her life.

What her dad should have done

1 Informed Tanya that, even if she hadn't thrown any rocks, if she stood there watching and laughing she was just as much to blame.

2 Ensure that Tanya made a full and genuine apology to the owner of the service station.

3 Ensure that Tanya paid back her share of the damages. (This would mean she would need to find a job and earn the money herself.)

4 When, and only when, the money was repaid would she be free to happily — and hopefully more wisely — go on with her life.

Yasmin, aged 11, shoplifting

Yasmin had been struggling to fit in at her new school, and one afternoon she had gone with one of the 'bad girls' from her year and been caught stealing some perfume from a department store. The store detective had been watching them acting obviously suspiciously for about 10 minutes before he saw them slip the perfume into their bags. He nabbed them as they tried to leave the store. When her dad arrived, she was sobbing and clearly under the impression that she was going to jail.

What her dad did

Basically, nothing. He was so distraught at seeing her so distraught that he simply cuddled her, told her everything was going to be OK, and took her home. On the way they stopped for some McDonald's, because he wanted to take her mind off this clearly very upsetting event. He tried to talk to her in the car, but she'd started to cry all over again, so he just let the whole thing slip quietly into the warm and comforting embrace of wilful ignorance.

What her dad should have done

1 Reassured her that she wasn't going to jail, but that the situation was very serious, and that he was upset with her, and she had let herself down.

2 Make her apologize to the department store manager.

3 Institute a suitably appropriate punishment (eg, loss of privileges like computer time or television time).

4 Once it had all calmed down, talk to her about her problems at school, and help her to figure out for herself why she had got involved with shoplifting (which is probably that she was just trying to impress the other girl) and what she could have done differently.

5 Tell her that everyone makes mistakes, but the important thing is to learn from them and move on.

Tips on Bad girls

☆ Don't panic.

☆ Don't get too angry.

☆ Let her feel the consequences fully.

☆ Seek wise counsel, not clever counsel.

☆ Model respect.

☆ Compassion is good; idiot compassion not so good.

23

Separation and divorce — when good love goes bad

Some people should never meet, they should never have a first date, but if they did they should definitely not have a second date. We've seen countless examples of this played out in public as various celebrities' relationships burn up on national television, and it's so much worse when their kids get caught up in all the craziness. This is nothing new, though, because adults have been behaving like idiots in situations like this since time immemorial. It was squabbling parents who led King Solomon to suggest cutting a baby in half to resolve a custody dispute. It's been said that this was an incredibly wise act, but it's also possible ole King Solomon was a bit of a nutcase and was just fed up with all the whining.

I've met warring parents who, if they'd been presented with that choice, would almost certainly have started arguing about who should get the top half.

After many years spent working in the Family Court, I came to understand why King Solomon could have got to the point that he did. Except my urge was not so much to chop up children as it was to slap their parents senseless. I would have clapped and cheered if just once, in the middle of petty and ridiculous Family Court hearings, the judge had told the parents to shut the fuck up, grow the fuck up, and sort their shit out.

No judge ever has, and likely ever will, but I guarantee they feel like saying it.

I have seen it in their eyes.

More dads are getting sole or joint custody of their daughters

History is a funny old thing: it seems to flip, and flip, and flip again, and we're none the wiser. During the 1990s, a raft of fathers groups sprung up to champion the rights of dads against what they saw as a mother-biased system. Whilst it's true that mothers were more likely to get custody of the children, this hasn't always been the case. For example, in the United States in the early 19th century it was quite common practice for the father to be awarded custody so that he could both provide for the children and look after their religious and secular education, and it wasn't until the industrial revolution kicked in, which took fathers out of the home and into factories, when the balance began to shift. It was when mothers were then left increasingly in sole charge of the children during the day that the concept of the 'maternal bond' began to gain a foothold. Once it did, though, it did so with a vengeance, and for a long time the pendulum swung back the other way, with mothers routinely being awarded custody in the vast majority of cases.

The fathers' rights groups were born out of a sense of frustration that men were not being accorded an equal opportunity to play an active role in their children's lives. This position was backed up by an increasing body of research in the 1980s and 1990s which showed that fathers were just as able as mothers to provide for the care and welfare of their children. The developing scientific picture now very clearly demonstrates that the outcomes for children are largely the same, whether they are placed with their mother or their father. There are some minor differences in outcomes for particular aspects of later adjustment, but the big picture is that — on balance — kids do just as well with their dads as they do with their mums. There are studies which show that kids living in single-father houses are more at risk of some things; but countering that, the same studies show that kids living in single-mother households are more at risk of other things. I'm not going to list all those things off here, because it just gets confusing and, I believe, unnecessarily worrying because the broad trends aren't really all that important. In fact, that stuff is generally the blunt instrument that people use to further their argument when they're standing in front of a Family Court judge.

Don't pay too much heed to this when you hear it. In my view, the important thing is that, when all the swings and roundabouts have been swung and rounded-about, dads are just as capable of being the sole caregivers for their daughters and sons as mums.

What hurts them most

What we do know — and we know this convincingly and beyond the shadow of any doubt — is that the thing which hurts children the most is exposure to adult conflict. This one is a no-brainer, but it constantly amazes me how many parents who profess to love their children dearly will expose them to absolutely horrible levels of conflict, all in the name of who's right and who's wrong. I remember Oprah Winfrey once said: 'Do you want to be right, or do you want to be happy?' If you were to rethink this one for the separation game, the question would be: 'Do you want to be right, or do you want your kids to be happy?' Be in no doubt that if you expose your kids to adult conflict then you are going to mess them up. You will also be putting them at higher risk of all kinds of antisocial and self-harming behaviours. Normally I'm not into trying to make parents feel guilty, but if you play any role in your kids being exposed to this sort of crap then you bloody should feel guilty.

Golden rules for healthy separations

These are my suggestions for how best to manage a separation when there are children involved. Again, I'm not usually one for telling people things like 'If you don't do it my way, your children will be damaged', but this is the one area where I make an exception to that rule. The reason for this is that the science is clearly on my side here, and it's one of those rare areas in psychology where we all agree, plus I've seen too many kids made miserable by parents who couldn't get their shit together. So do it my way.

◇ *The children's best interests are paramount*
Whatever you do, you must always make sure that what's motivating you is the children's best interests. Sometimes it might be hard to be objective about this, but you have to work very hard to do that. Take objective advice, and listen to it.

◇ *Keep the conflict away from the children*
If you don't, you *will* hurt them — and you'll be behaving like an immature, selfish git. So don't.

◇ *If their mother is the one who engages in conflict, simply rise above it and don't bite*
No matter what she throws at you, stand firm and keep sight of the fact that it doesn't matter what she says or does — all that matters is that you're being a good dad and not engaging in petty fighting.

◇ *Always be positive about her mother around your daughter*
Never put her mother down. Even if you have reason — in fact, *especially* if you have reason — never put her mother down. It does your daughter no good to have you criticize her mum.

◇ *Work as hard as you can to build a strong co-parenting relationship with her mother*
You may not like each other very much, but you will continue

to be parents to your daughter as long as you're both alive, so dig in and do everything you can to let your daughter see that you and her mum are still the stable corners of her world.

◊ *Sort out any matrimonial property stuff as quickly and as fairly as you can*
   If your girl's mother left you, this can often be a way to 'get back' at her. Don't. Get in, get it sorted, and then both of you get on with your respective lives as quickly as you can.

The big issue here is that you have to work as hard as you can to ensure that you keep the adult stuff with the adults and the kid stuff with the kids. You might hate each other's respective guts, but you have a bigger responsibility to your children. You don't have the luxury of wallowing about in self-pity and anger — you're a dad. Wallow about in that stuff when your daughter isn't around. Sometimes you have to wallow a bit, because that's the only way through, but always remember that all that stuff is poison to your daughter. First and foremost you are a dad, and dad's protect their children from the bad stuff. It's as simple as that.

Dropkick mums

The idea that the maternal bond is a sacred, unbreakable thing is a nice idea, but sadly it doesn't always work out that way. Just as there are dropkick dads who abandon their kids, so too there are dropkick mums. This might seem like a bit of a harsh old term, but I don't think it is. I think if you abandon your kids, then you're a dropkick, plain and simple. There are all kinds of reasons people give for abandoning their children, but none of them really matter. All that matters is the fact that you have kids who have been abandoned by one of the two people in the world they should have been able to count on.

Sometimes dropkick mums will abandon their children outright, and other times they'll do it effectively by emotionally abandoning their kids. She might still see her daughter from time to time, but when she does it will be randomly, with plenty of broken promises and disappointments. Hopes will be raised and then dashed for no apparent reason. These kinds of mums will use all manner of excuses for why this happens, but the end result will always be the same: your daughter will be left feeling rejected and disappointed yet again.

If you find yourself in this position, here are my suggestions for how to help your daughter deal with this very difficult situation.

◊ Just keep talking. The nice thing about girls is that they do tend to talk about how they're feeling, so let her talk.

◊ Remember she may not want you to solve the problem. Men tend to approach conversations about problems with a 'how do we fix it' orientation. That's fine, but sometimes she just might want to talk about how it makes her feel upset. Give her room to do that when she needs to.

◊ Let her know that you know it sucks. You don't want to run down her mum, but you do want her to know that you know not having a mum around really sucks.

◊ Keep doing the basics. Most kids like routines and rules, and it will help her to know that, even though her mum might not be there, life will go on as usual.

◊ Problems aren't excuses. It's also important for her to understand that being upset about her mum's behaviour doesn't mean this is an excuse for her own bad behaviour. She needs to know that she is responsible for her own behaviour, just like her mother is responsible for her behaviour.

◊ Make sure she knows that you will always be there, and that you will always be on her side. Say it over and over.

◊ Cuddle her and tell her you love her as much as you can. Make sure she knows that her mum might not be there, but that you are — and that you know what an amazingly special person she is.

It's a difficult and painful thing for a parent to see their child hurting, no matter what the cause. It will probably make you feel angry and probably want to say unkind things about her mother. I understand that completely — but don't. It won't help her; it will only add to her burden. Just be there for her. That's all you have to do. Just be there.

Introducing your new 'special friend'

This one is a bit of a minefield, because if you have a new person enter your life it can be the start of all kinds of issues. The trick here is to exercise a little care and diplomacy, and try as hard as you can to pace it right. This is my standard advice for bringing a new 'special friend' into your and her lives.

◊ *Wait until the relationship is serious enough to warrant the potential stresses it might cause*
There's nothing to be gained from introducing every 'special friend' you date. Usually all this does is create problems as she sees a whole lot of new people coming and going.

◊ *Slow is best*
It's just plain old common sense that the best approach is a softly-softly one. Introduce the new person with caution and an understanding that everyone is going to need time to adjust.

◊ *Be clear about the roles with your new partner*
The newbie isn't a new mum, and shouldn't act or even think like that. The newbie is the newbie, and should be

treated with the respect given to any visitor in the house; anything else will need to be earned. Make sure your new partner understands that you are the parent and that it will likely be quite some time before they get to have a say in family matters.

◊ *Be prepared for a reaction*
It's likely that your girl is going to find it difficult having someone new come into the family, particularly someone she might feel is trying to replace her mum. Both you and your new partner need to be prepared for this.

◊ *Be tolerant, but don't be a punching bag*
Your daughter might get angry or upset, but she still needs to show you the same respect she always has. She needs to understand and accept that you have a right to a life of your own. This might take her a while, so in the meantime let her be angry, but not rude.

The thing which our children sometimes find hard to grasp is that we also have a right to a life. Sure, our primary duty is to them; but eventually they will move out and we'll be left with whatever's left after they're gone. 'Special friends' are great, and they can work out fine, you just have to make sure you show a little sensitivity and pacing when you're introducing them to your kids.

Tips on
Separation and divorce

☆ Exposing children to adult conflict is damaging.

☆ The child's wellbeing is the most important consideration.

☆ The child should be kept away from any conflict at all times.

☆ It is important to always be positive about the other parent, even if they aren't about you.

☆ Working hard to build a good co-parenting relationship with their mother is critical.

☆ If you do have a new 'friend', be mindful about when and how you introduce them into your daughter's life.

24

Take one dose of dad twice daily — why you are the best vaccine she has

Hopefully, something has been jumping out at you over the past few chapters. Think back to what the most recent science tells us about what puts girls at more risk for things like eating disorders, depression and anxiety, school problems, early sexual behaviour, delinquency, and all those other scary Marys, and you'll find the same usual suspects lurking around in the background. It almost always comes down to these same underlying factors every time bad things are happening to girls:

◊ absent father

◊ conflict with parents

◊ conflict between parents

◊ poor discipline in the home

◊ parents who are over-controlling or over-protective

◊ parents not being involved in her life

◊ low self-worth

◊ negative thoughts and feelings.

Remember, this isn't just stuff I pulled out of a hat to fill up pages: this is the stuff that the past four to five decades of research has confirmed over and over again. There is great comfort to be taken from this, because, whilst the issues themselves might be complex and multifaceted, the answer to how you can best protect her from them seems to be pretty simple.

I think it was Einstein who said that we should 'keep things as simple as possible, but no simpler'. Smart guy. Researchers and clinicians will probably go on debating forever the finer points of what causes girls to develop eating disorders, or get depressed, or start having sex at 13, but none of that really matters to you and your girl. All that matters is that you now know what you need to do to vaccinate her against all these things.

Just for the record, so you can tick them off against your own list, here's my take on how to do that.

◇ *Be involved in her life*
   It is fundamentally important that you are involved in her life, and that she feels you're interested in her and her world. Girls want their dads to be interested in them — they don't want you to back away when it all gets a little bit confusing.

◇ *Make her feel loved*
   It's obvious, I know. And I know I've said it before, but it's so important I'm going to say it again: make her feel loved. It is the single most powerful thing you can do for her, and it will help to keep her safe through all manner of trials.

◇ *Model respectful relationships with women*
   You will be her first and most important teacher in showing her what she should expect from men. You need to be the kind of man you want her to marry. It's clichéd advice, but it's no less true for that. If you're with her mother, then be a good man. If you're separated, then be a good man and treat her mother with respect 100% of the time. If you're with someone else, treat her with respect. Your daughter will look to you to see how it's done, so show her.

◇ *Provide rules*

Just like all of us, she needs rules and boundaries. This means that inevitably there will be times when she says that she doesn't like you very much. That's fine; she'll always love you, and that's what really counts. Rules are how you do your bit to keep her safe. Rules are how you help her to learn that actions have consequences. Rules are how you show her that you love her.

◇ *Give her room to grow*

This is the balancing act, the other side of the coin. Just as she needs rules and boundaries, and someone watching out for her, she also needs room to roam the world and find stuff out for herself. You can protect her from many things, but not from everything, and so she needs to practise life before she heads out on her own. This is a hard one, but it's important as well. You won't get it right all of the time, but that's OK because none of us do. You just do the best you can.

◇ *Help her to deal with difficult feelings*

This is far easier than it sounds. A lot of it is just listening to her — *really* listening, not just sitting there quietly. Some if it is helping her to understand what the young have yet to learn: that eventually all things pass. With time, most hurts heal, and even the ones that never fully heal simply become a comfortable scar.

◇ *Teach her to believe in herself*

The best way to do this is to model it. If you believe in her, then she will too. This doesn't mean you have to blindly trust her to figure things out for herself. Instead, what it means is that you believe that, with a little time, a little help, and some trial and error, she'll get there in the end. If you tell her you believe in her, then she will too. There will be plenty of times when she feels lost and confused, as do we all, but in those times your job is to sit with her quietly and tell her she just needs to keep going and she'll figure it out. She always does.

See, the whole book just got boiled down to four pages. Shame you didn't read this bit first and you could have skipped all that other stuff, eh?

Tips on
Your being the best vaccine

☆ Be involved in her life.

☆ Make her feel loved.

☆ Model respectful relationships with women.

☆ Provide rules.

☆ Help her deal with difficult feelings.

☆ Give her room to grow.

☆ Teach her to believe in herself.

25

How to be a cool dad

When I wrote the mums' version of this chapter in *Mothers Raising Sons*, it was a lot longer and there were a lot more bullet points. It occurs to me that probably feminists looking at these two books will draw the conclusion that, once again, we men are trying to make it much harder for mums than dads. I suppose that's possible — most things are possible after all — but I'm not consciously setting out to do that. Instead, I think it's just different. Boys are into doing stuff, they like to do things. Girls on the other hand seem to like just being around, and feeling like they matter to their dads.

There's another difference, too, because for the mums I said that this chapter was optional, it was like dessert. None of it was essential, but it would probably make things more fun. For dads it's a bit different, because I think all of these things *are* essential. I think they're all compulsory. So to make sure that you don't get overloaded with a whole lot of extra stuff that you have to do, I've boiled it down to three simple things (yes, three!) you just need to repeat over and over, as much as you can, through all the days of her life.

1. Invite her into your life

To make girls feel special, you need to invite them into your life.

She will love you just as much if you don't, but that love will inevitably be tinged with a slight sadness, a barely perceptible feeling that she never quite knew who you were. Yet if you invite her in, she will know you from the inside out. It isn't even very hard to do, because I mean literally invite her into your life. Take her with you to work from time to time. If you work in an office, let her ride the lifts and spin in your chair. If you drive a truck, let her ride in the cab from time to time. If you work in a warehouse, let her come and ride in the forklift or scoot around the aisles. (Obviously you'll need to do this carefully and also when the safety nazis aren't watching.) Whatever your job is, she's going to think it's cool.

If you're a muso, let her listen to your band play, or your orchestra, or whatever it is you do. If you're a hunter, or a fisherman, or a tramper, take her with you into the great outdoors. Pack her up in boots and woollen jerseys and gloves and scarves and watch the sun come up over some river or mountain. She will remember days like that forever. Let her watch you make wooden furniture in the shed if that's your thing. Let her pass you the socket wrench if cars are your thing. Whatever your thing is, take her along and show her the stuff you get passionate about.

Take her out for coffees and conversation, or fish and chips and a chat. Take her with you when you're walking to the corner store to buy a newspaper on a Sunday morning. Go on as many holidays with her as time and money allow. These are the things that she will remember.

Whatever you do, and wherever you do it, invite her in as often as you can.

2. Visit her in hers

As I said earlier, you don't have to spend your life having tea parties, but you should do it from time to time. (You might be surprised at how much fun that stuff can be. Of course I'm guessing here, having never been to one myself, but I'm simply saying it's possible) As she gets older it will be important to find things you can do together, and it's important that at least some of those things are of her choosing. If she's into sports or music then it's much easier, because you can be the dad who is always there for every game he can, the dad who comes to every concert. Whatever it is she's into, you get into it too. It's obvious, I know, but you'd be surprised how many parents have other more important stuff to do than be at their daughter's soccer match.

None of us is perfect, we all get tied up in our own lives and work. Yesterday, I missed my younger son's last soccer match of the season because I had to get this book written. They lost 2–1, and apparently it was a really close game because both teams hadn't lost a game all season. Here's the thing, though, here's the stinger: I already know that when I'm an old bloke, and when he's off in his own life doing his own thing, I'll feel much worse about missing that game than I would for not finishing this book on time.

As your daughter gets older, her interests will change, and you must change with them. Every so often you may need to take her shopping for a morning and suffer the living death of shoe stores. There's no way around it, though, because it has to be done. Besides, afterwards you'll get to sit down with her and have coffee and a chat about the comings and goings of her world.

Surely that's worth a few bloody shoe stores?

3. It's the little things that matter

If you think about it, the moments in our lives that seem to shine the brightest are often about the smallest simple things. It might be a memory of her laughing at a clown when she was four, or a day with a mate out fishing, or when your own dad said some small thing to you and it made you feel like the biggest little man on Earth. So it is with her, too, because the little things are always the things that we remember. Tell her jokes, cuddle her as much and often as you can, sing her silly songs, leave her notes telling her how proud you are of her — all these things and whatever else you can think of. Obviously you don't need to do this stuff constantly, because you'll probably drive her crazy, but make sure you sprinkle little magic moments throughout her life. They will fill her up just as much at 35 as they did at five.

Tips on
How to be a cool dad

☆ Invite her into your life.

☆ Visit her in hers.

☆ Always remember that it's the little things that matter.

26

Zombies and high heels (a reprise)

Here's how you want it to go down.

No one could have foreseen the end of the world as we know it, except of course all the people who'd spent the last 30 years watching zombie movies. They would have just nodded their heads and gone: 'Yeah, well obviously.'

Still, most of them were dead now, eaten alive by the shuffling hordes of undead, who, just like Romero predicted all those years ago, really did have a thing for living human brains.

Small pockets of survivors have managed to find safety. Some of them in office blocks, some in boats, and some in shopping malls. That's what your daughter did. She knew straight away that it was all coming undone, and, rather than sitting about like a stunned monkey waiting for the end, she jumped into a truck and drove her way through the ambling dead to this place: the Uber-Mall.

Along the way, she picked up a few others as well: a pregnant lady, a cop, a biker dude, an old guy and his wife, and a man who looked like he used to make a living selling dodgy real-estate deals to old people.

It had all gone fairly well to begin with, because they'd backed the truck up to the rear delivery yard, shot the lock out with the cop's .40-calibre Glock pistol, and then charged inside, bolting the door just before chattery-toothed zombies started clawing at the door with their decaying fingers.

Steve, the dodgy real-estate guy, had sat down, mopping his head with a stained yellow handkerchief as everyone else stood around looking a bit stunned.

It's now that your daughter takes charge, because she knows that when you're surrounded by thousands of flesh-eating zombies it's no time to stand around feeling sorry for yourself.

'We need to fan out and check that the place is clear before we do anything else,' she says. 'Let's get a secure perimeter before we start thinking about putting our feet up.'

The biker guy, who's got the crappiest attitude to women you could ever hope to find, simply giggles nervously. (Not a fetching look for an overweight greasy man dressed in leather.) 'Listen to her. Why don't you just take a chill pill, bitch?'

Your daughter, who does not take such things quietly, hardly misses a beat. She marches right up to him and leans in so close that she can see the sweat leaking from him. 'You hear that sound?' she asks him. 'That's the noise that thousands of hungry freaks make when they're going out of their tiny monster minds, scratching and chewing their way through anything that looks like it might be a way into this place, because all they really want to do is tear you apart while you're still screaming. So you think we should take a chill pill, or do you think we should make sure that all the doors and windows are closed?'

Biker guy swallows, but says nothing.

'I thought so,' she says. 'Let's spread out.'

It doesn't take long. While she's looking out the back of a large hardware store, she hears a scream and two gunshots. More screaming now.

'Shit.'

Taking the axe she'd picked up when she first entered the hardware store, she sprints out into the mall forecourt. Sure enough, there's one of the hungry freaks sitting astride the dodgy real-estate guy, ripping his throat out with its teeth. Blood sprays over the white marble floor like bad special-effects. The pregnant lady is collapsed back against the fountain, frozen in fear. The screaming comes from the biker guy, who is just standing there like a big, greasy dummy.

From the corner of her eye, your daughter sees the cop. 'Shoot it!' she yells.

The cop points his Glock and fires off two rounds, both hitting the undead crazy in the body. All that seems to do is piss it off, and it swings around, glaring at the cop, dripping blood and leftover bad real-estate deals. The cop fires again, hitting the zombie dead-centre with three more rounds.

'No!' she yells, but the cop isn't listening now because, almost quicker than the eye can follow, the zombie is up and sprinting at him at full-speed.

'You have to shoot it in the—' she yells, but more rounds drown out her words.

She knows what's going to happen, sees it in slow-motion, as she turns towards the cop. The creature hits him at full-speed, knocking the Glock spinning away across the floor, and both of them go down in a flailing tangle of limbs and teeth. There's more screaming, and more bad special-effects.

Without missing a beat, your girl sprints over, raising her axe as she runs. 'Hey, freak boy?' she yells.

The zombie looks up, and the naked hunger in its eyes is almost enough to throw her focus.

Almost, but not quite.

She brings the axe down in a single powerful arc that splits its head open in one stroke, grimacing as a spray of cold red slime splashes her face.

The zombie falls dead, this time *dead* dead. All-gone-and-never-coming-back dead.

She stands there, panting for a moment, trying to get her breath back.

'Holy shit!' a voice comes from behind her, the biker. 'You killed it.'

'You have to destroy their brains,' she says. 'Shooting them in the chest won't stop them. You need to shoot them in the head.'

'Where did you learn that?' he asks, slightly in awe of what he's just seen.

She turns to face him, dripping zombie blood and brains, but with eyes that are strong and clear. She smiles then, and simply says: 'My dad.'

Would that be cool?

Shit yeah, it would be cool.

So get busy, you've got a girl to grow.

Good luck.

Endnotes

Chapter 1
15 Perhaps not surprisingly, there have been numerous studies
L Nielson (2005). Fathers and daughters: a needed course in family
studies. *Marriage and Family Review* 38(3), 1–13.

Chapter 4
33 In a particularly revealing study   LK Hagan and J Kuebli
(2007). Mothers' and fathers' socialization of preschoolers' physical
risk taking. *Journal of Applied Developmental Psychology* 28, 2–14.

Chapter 6
46 I've written about that elsewhere   Nigel Latta (2009).
Mothers Raising Sons. HarperCollins: Auckland.

46 What is pretty obvious   Judith Kleinfeld (2009). The state of
American boyhood. *Gender Issues* 26(2), 113–129.

47 It was grim and frightening stuff   Sharon R Mazzarella
and Norma O Pecora (2007). Girls in crisis: newspaper coverage of
adolescent girls. *Journal of Communication Inquiry* 31(1), 6–27.

Chapter 7
51 And there have been some very cool-sounding   C Fine
(2008). Will working mothers' brains explode? The popular new
genre of neurosexism. *Neuroethics* 1(1), 69–72. Or you can find a link
to download a copy of this paper at http://www.cordeliafine.com/
academic_work.html.

52 This term isn't mine   Mark Liberman (2008). Sexual
pseudoscience on CNN. http://languagelog.ldc.upenn.edu/
nll/?p=260.

53 Recent studies using MRI scans   Leonard Sax (2001).
Rethinking Title IX. *The Washington Times*, 2 June 2001, A17; http://
www.singlesexschools.org/links-washtimes.htm.

53 The girl brain circuits   Louann Brizendine (2007). *The Female Brain*. Bantam Books: London, at p 61.

54 All you need to do   DS Weisberg (2008). Caveat lector: the presentation of neuroscience information in the popular media. *The Scientific Review of Mental Health Practice* 6(1), 51–56.

54 To their credit   DS Weisberg *et al* (2008). The seductive allure of neuroscience explanations. *Journal of Cognitive Neuroscience*, 20(3), 470–477.

56 Sure there is   M Layne Kalbfleisch (2008). Getting to the heart of the brain: using cognitive neuroscience to explore the nature of human ability and performance. *Roeper Review* 30, 162–170.

57 If neuroscientists are to prevent their work   JT Bruer (2002). Avoiding the pediatrician's error: how neuroscientists can help educators (and themselves). *Nature Neuroscience* 5 Suppl, 1031–1033.

58 Some authors have claimed   Leonard Sax (2006). *Why gender matters: what teachers and parents need to know about the emerging science of single sex education*. Bantam: New York.

58 If you want to see the whole argument   Mark Liberman (2008). Liberman on Sax on Liberman on Sax on hearing. http://languagelog.ldc.upenn.edu/nll/?p=171.

60 We're told that these differences   Leonard Sax (2006). *Why gender matters: what teachers and parents need to know about the emerging science of single sex education*. Bantam: New York.

60 And would it surprise you   Mark Liberman (2008). Retinal sex and sexual rhetoric. http://languagelog.ldc.upenn.edu/nll/?p=174.

61 Well, this statement   William DS Killgore *et al* (2001). Sex-specific developmental changes in amygdala responses to affective faces. *Neuro Report* 12(2), 427–433. Or online at http://ldc.upenn.edu/myl/llog/KillgoreAmygdala.pdf.

62 The only problem   Mark Liberman (2006). Are men emotional children? http://158.130.17.5/~myl/languagelog/archives/003284.html.

62 Having said that   Matthias R Mehl *et al* (2007). Are women really more talkative than men? *Science* 317, 82.

63   Indeed, several large studies   Janet S Hyde and Janet E Mertz (2009). Gender, culture, and mathematics performance. *Proceedings of the National Academy of Science of the United States of America* 106(22), 8801–8807.

Chapter 8
67   All that aside   Janet Shibley Hyde (2005). The gender similarities hypothesis. *American Psychologist* 60(6), 581–592.

Chapter 9
76   It's now fairly well accepted   A Caspi *et al* (2005). Personality development: stability and change. *Annual Reviews of Psychology* 56, 453–484.

78   This doesn't mean   David P Schmidt *et al* (2008). Why can't a man be more like a woman? Sex differences in big five personality traits across 55 cultures. *Journal of Personality and Social Psychology* 94(1), 168–182.

80   I've included in the endnotes   The Dunedin Multidisciplinary Health and Development Research Unit's webpage features all kinds of information about the amazing things the DMDHDR has spent nearly four decades uncovering. It's well worth a look: http://dunedinstudy.otago.ac.nz/.

81   Researchers at the DMDHDS   A Caspi *et al* (2003). Children's behavioural styles at age 3 are linked to their adult personality traits at age 26. *Journal of Personality* 71(4), 495–514.

86   What should be at least   T Klimstra *et al* (2009). Maturation of personality in adolescence. *Journal of Personality and Social Psychology* 96(4), 898–912.

Chapter 10
90   There are a number of studies   Thomas Spielhofer *et al* (2004). A study of the effects of school size and single-sex education in English schools. *Research Papers in Education* 19(2), 133–159.

90   There are also studies   S Billiger (2009). On restructuring school segregation: the efficacy and equity of single-sex schooling. *Economics of Education Review* 28(3), 393–402.

91   When you take all those differences   Pamela Robinson and
Alan Smithers (1999). Should the sexes be separated for secondary
education — comparisons of single-sex and co-educational schools.
Research Papers in Education 14(1), 23–49.

91   One theme that does seem   Peter Daly and Neil Defty (2004).
Extension of single-sex public school provision: evidential concerns.
Evaluation and Research in Education, 18(1–2), 129–136. Alice Sullivan
(2009). Academic self-concept, gender and single-sex schooling.
British Educational Research Journal 35(2), 259–288.

Chapter 11
99   It could well be   Jessica Ringrose (2006). A new universal
mean girl: examining the discursive construction and social
regulation of a new feminine pathology. *Feminism & Psychology* 16(4),
405–424.

100   High-status girls   L Mayeux and AHN Cillessen (2008).
It's not just being popular, it's knowing it, too: the role of self-
perceptions of status in the associations between peer status and
aggression. *Social Development* 17(4), 871–888.

100 . . . and the impact   EK Willer and WR Cupach (2008). When
'sugar and spice' turn to 'fire and ice': factors affecting the adverse
consequences of relational aggression among adolescent girls.
Communication Studies 59, 415–429.

100   In fact, just the presence   D Murray-Close and JM Ostrov
(2009). A longitudinal study of forms and functions of aggressive
behavior in early childhood. *Child Development* 80, 828–842.

100   Of course   Nicole Heilbron and Mitchell J Prinstein (2008).
A review and reconceptualization of social aggression: adaptive and
maladaptive correlates. *Clinical Child and Family Psychology Review*
11(4), 176–217.

Chapter 14
125   There are now a number   JM Tither and BJ Ellis (2008).
Impact of fathers on daughters' age of menarche: a genetically and
environmentally controlled sibling study. *Developmental Psychology*
44(5), 1409–1420.

125 The better mum   D Saxbe and RL Repetti (2009). Fathers' and mothers' marital relationship predicts daughters' pubertal development two years later. *Journal of Adolescence* 32(2), 415–423.

Chapter 15
138 The ugly truth is   CL Sisk and DL Foster (2004). The neural basis of puberty and adolescence. *Nature Neuroscience* 7(10), 1040–1047.

140 We've all probably heard   KD Schwartz (2008). Adolescent brain development: an oxymoron no longer. *Journal of Youth Ministry* 6(2), 85–93.

140 One of those interesting things   JN Giedd *et al* (1999). Brain development during adolescence: a longitudinal MRI study. *Nature Neuroscience* 2(10), 861–863.

141 Not only is there a lot   RK Lenroot and JN Giedd (2006). Brain development in children and adolescents: insights from anatomical magnetic resonance imaging. *Neuroscience and Biobehavioral Review* 30(6), 718–729.

141 What has only recently been discovered   Jay N Giedd *et al* (2009). Anatomical brain magnetic resonance imaging of typically developing children and adolescents. *Journal of the American Academy of Child and Adolescent Psychiatry* 48(5), 465–470.

143 As one concrete example   RF McGivern *et al* (2002). Cognitive efficiency on a match to a simple task decreases at the onset of puberty in children. *Brain and Cognition* 50(1), 73–89.

143 Neurons are great   SJ Blakemore (2007). Brain development during adolescence. *Education Review* 20(1), 82–90.

146 While they might know   Laurence Steinberg (2005). Cognitive and affective development in adolescence. *Trends in Cognitive Neuroscience* 9(2), 69–74.

147 The end result   LD Steinberg (2007). Risk taking in adolescence: new perspectives from brain and behavioral science. *Current Directions in Psychological Science* 16(2), 55–59.

Chapter 18
178   In 1997, some of the researchers   L Magdol *et al* (1997).
Gender differences in partner violence in a birth cohort of 21-year-olds: bridging the gap between clinical and epidemiological approaches. *Journal of Consulting and Clinical Psychology* 65(1), 68–78.

179   So it was that 11 years later   DM Fergusson *et al* (2008).
Developmental antecedents of interpartner violence in a New Zealand birth cohort. *Journal of Family Violence* 23, 737–753.

181   Female violence has likely   Katherine P Luke (2008). Are girls really becoming more violent? A critical analysis. *Affilia* 23(1), 38-50.

181   For a long time   Christie Barron and Dany Lacombe (2005).
Moral panic and the nasty girl. *Canadian Review of Sociology and Anthropology* 42(1), 51–69.

Chapter 19
185   It's also important for you   AL May *et al* (2006). Parent–adolescent relationships and the development of weight concerns from early to late adolescence. *International Journal of Eating Disorders* 39(8), 729–740.

188   This isn't as rare   Lien Goossens *et al* (2009). Prevalence and characteristics of binge eating in an adolescent community sample. *Journal of Clinical Child and Adolescent Psychology* 38(3), 342–353.

189   Whilst there has been a steady increase   C Sancho *et al* (2007). Epidemiology of eating disorders: A two year follow up in an early adolescent school population. *European Child and Adolescent Psychiatry* 16, 495–504.

189   This is now the most common   JJ Thomas *et al* (2009).
The relationship between eating disorders not otherwise specified (EDNOS) and officially recognized eating disorders: meta-analysis and implications for DSM. *Psychological Bulletin* 135 (3), 407–433.

192   Researchers are still arguing   Yael Latzer *et al* S (2009).
Marital and parent–child relationships in families with daughters who have eating disorders. *Journal of Family Issues* 30(9), 1201–1220.
AL May *et al* (2006). Parent–adolescent relationships and the development of weight concerns from early to late adolescence. *International Journal of Eating Disorders* 39(8), 729–740.

195 The more she feels accepted   Ciara McEwen and Eirini Flouri (2009). Fathers' parenting, adverse life events, and adolescents' emotional and eating disorder symptoms: the role of emotion regulation. *European Journal of Child and Adolescent Psychiatry* 18(4), 206–216.

195 In one longitudinal study   WS Agras *et al* (2007). Childhood risk factors for thin body preoccupation and social pressure to be thin. *Journal of the American Academy of Child and Adolescent Psychiatry* 46(2), 171–178.

195 Interestingly, some researchers have found   R Rodgers and H Chabrol (2009). Parental attitudes, body image disturbance and disordered eating amongst adolescents and young adults: a review. *European Eating Disorders Review* 17(2), 137–151.

197 Just as we know a lot more   WS Agras and AH Robinson (2008). Forty years of progress in the treatment of eating disorders. *Nordic Journal of Psychiatry* 62 Suppl 47, 19–24.

Chapter 20
198 The reason for this may be   NK Eberhart *et al* (2006). Understanding the sex difference in vulnerability to adolescent depression: an examination of child and parent characteristics. *Journal of Abnormal Child Psychology* 34(4), 495–508.

199 They affect large numbers   E Karevold *et al* (2009). Predictors and pathways from infancy to symptoms of anxiety and depression in early adolescence. *Developmental Psychology* 45(4), 1051–1060.

199 It seems that the common thread   PJ Tully *et al* (2009). The structure of anxiety and depression in a normative sample of younger and older Australian adolescents. *Journal of Abnormal Child Psychology* 37(5), 717–726.

199 It also seems that   MV Snyman *et al* (2003). Young adolescent girls' experience of non-clinical depression. *Education* 124(2), 269–288.

200 It probably won't surprise you to learn   A Sourander *et al* (2006). Early predictors of deliberate self-harm among adolescents: a prospective follow-up study from age 3 to age 15. *Journal of Affective Disorders* 93(1–3), 87–96.

201 **In a very large international study**   G Scoliers *et al* (2009). Reasons for adolescent deliberate self-harm: a cry of pain and/or a cry for help — findings from the child and adolescent self-harm in Europe (CASE) study. *Social Psychiatry and Psychiatric Epidemiology* 44(8), 601–607.

202 **It seems that there are a number**   H Fliege *et al* (2009). Risk factors and correlates of deliberate self-harm behaviour: a systematic review. *Journal of Psychosomatic Research* 66(6), 477–493.

Chapter 21

207 **One Scottish study**   Suzanne C Penfold *et al* (2009). Factors associated with self-reported first sexual intercourse in Scottish adolescents. *BMC Research Notes* 2(42), 1–6.

207 **Except it gets even more interesting**   K Kaye *et al* (2009). Parent marital quality and the parent-adolescent relationship: effects on sexual activity amongst adolescents and youth. *Marriage and Family Review* 45(2–3), 189–217.

207 **... but having an absent father**   BJ Ellis *et al* (2003). Does father absence place daughters at special risk for early sexual activity and teenage pregnancy? *Child Development* 74(3), 801–821.

207 **Even more interesting still**   Rebekah L Coley *et al* (2009). Fathers' and mothers' parenting predicting and responding to adolescent sexual risk behaviours. *Child Development* 80(3), 808–827.

Chapter 22

215 **In 2001, some of the researchers published**   Terrie E Moffitt *et al* (2001). *Sex Differences in Antisocial Behaviour: conduct disorder, delinquency, and violence in the Dunedin longitudinal study.* Cambridge University Press: Cambridge.

Chapter 23

227 **It was when mothers were then left**   S Brown (2007). Why daddy loses. *Journal of Contemporary Legal Issues* 16, 177–180.

227 **This position was backed up**   R Warshak (1986). Father custody and child development: a review and analysis of psychological research. *Behavioral Sciences and the Law* 4, 185–202.

227 There are some minor differences in outcomes Mieke
Van Houtte and An Jacobs (2004). Consequences of the sex of the
custodial parent on three indicators of adolescents' well-being:
evidence from the Belgian data. *Journal of Divorce and Remarriage* 41,
143–163.

228 There are studies which show that kids Kyrre Breivik and
Dan Olweus (2006). Adolescent's adjustment in four post-divorce
family structures: single mother, stepfather, joint physical custody
and single father families. *Journal of Divorce and Remarriage* 44,
99–124.

228 What we do know Nicole M Bing *et al* (2009). Comparing
the effects of amount of conflict on children's adjustment following
parental divorce. *Journal of Divorce and Remarriage* 50, 159–171.